"Alice Fryling's valuable insights from the Enneagram and Scripture invite us to experience God's grace more deeply through greater self-awareness and spiritual companionship. This book is a rich and unique contribution to Enneagram literature and to personal transformation."
Richard Rohr, OFM, author of *The Enneagram: A Christian Perspective*

"This will be a most helpful resource for all who are seeking deeper levels of transformation through the narrow gate of self-knowledge and self-examination. Having worked with the Enneagram as a tool for transformation for many years, I love everything about this book—the concise descriptions of the history and theory of the Enneagram, the penetrating commentary on the spaces themselves, and the wise and gentle encouragement for how you can move from the bondage of the false self to the freedom of living as your true self in Christ. The personal meditations, discussion questions, and guidance for utilizing the Enneagram in spiritual direction make this enormously beneficial for personal and ministry use."
Ruth Haley Barton, founder, Transforming Center, author of *Sacred Rhythms*

"For many years, the Enneagram has helped many to understand their tendencies, strengths, and weaknesses. Now Alice Fryling has provided a very helpful guide for its use. I especially like the way she begins with an understandable explanation of the Enneagram and also matches personality types with Scripture meditations. I commend *Mirror for the Soul* to individuals seeking to understand how God has shaped them and to spiritual guides for their ministry with others."
Leighton Ford, president, Leighton Ford Ministries, Charlotte, North Carolina

"The Enneagram has both informed and matured my spiritual walk for more than twenty years now, and I am thrilled to see more Christians embracing its ancient wisdom. Whether you are new to the Enneagram or already a devotee, you will love *Mirror for the Soul*. It's as inspiring as it is insightful. Alice Fryling is a gifted guide. Take the journey with her, dig deep into its truth, and allow it to enhance your life. I loved this book and heartily recommend it."

Deb Hirsch, church leader and speaker, author of *Redeeming Sex*, coauthor of *Untamed*

"For many years, Alice has been a trustworthy guide for those who seek to love God and neighbor. *Mirror for the Soul* offers practical ways to engage with the Spirit for transformation through the tool of the Enneagram. We can't change what we aren't aware of. *Mirror for the Soul* can be both eye opening and healing. If you are hungry to grow in loving God and loving your neighbor as yourself, I commend this book to you. Its wisdom can reveal your default settings, hidden agendas, and besetting temptations, as well as the shimmering beauty of your soul. Breathe deep, lean hard; God's love holds."

Adele Calhoun, copastor of spiritual formation, Highrock Church, and author of *Spiritual Disciplines Handbook*

"This is the Enneagram book I've been looking for. It's written from a depth of experience, a depth in Scripture, and with an eye for the formational possibilities of this ancient wisdom. Fryling serves as a seasoned spiritual director, guiding the reader into the rich growth in spiritual formation that the Enneagram offers."

Alan Fadling, president and founder, Unhurried Living, author of *An Unhurried Leader*

"I've been waiting for this book! When I began studying the Enneagram ten years ago, Alice Fryling's insights set some key themes of my understanding of this enormously helpful tool in moving toward transformation to Christlikeness. Thank you!"

Jan Johnson, author of *Meeting God in Scripture* and *Renovation of the Heart in Daily Practice*

"The Enneagram points out where we are in need of grace; Christianity and Scripture point us in the direction where grace can be found. Alice Fryling's book is at the crossroads where the Enneagram and Christianity meet. Fryling brings understanding and transformation together in a very readable practical way."

Jerome Wagner, author of *Enneagram Spectrum of Personality Styles* and *Nine Lenses on the World*

Mirror
for the
SOUL

A Christian Guide
to the
Enneagram

Alice Fryling

IVP Books
An imprint of InterVarsity Press
Downers Grove, Illinois

InterVarsity Press
P.O. Box 1400, Downers Grove, IL 60515-1426
ivpress.com
email@ivpress.com

©2017 by Alice Fryling

*InterVarsity Press® is the book-publishing division of InterVarsity Christian Fellowship/USA®, a
movement of students and faculty active on campus at hundreds of universities, colleges, and schools of nursing
in the United States of America, and a member movement of the International Fellowship of Evangelical
Students. For information about local and regional activities, visit intervarsity.org.*

*All Scripture quotations, unless otherwise indicated, are taken from THE HOLY BIBLE,
NEW INTERNATIONAL VERSION®, NIV® Copyright © 1973, 1978, 1984, 2011 by Biblica, Inc.™
Used by permission. All rights reserved worldwide.*

*While any stories in this book are true, some names and identifying information may have been changed
to protect the privacy of individuals.*

Cover design: Cindy Kiple
Interior design: Jeanna Wiggins
Images: old mirror: © Jill Ferry/Getty Images

ISBN 978-0-8308-4632-0 (print)
ISBN 978-0-8308-9092-7 (digital)

Printed in the United States of America ∞

Library of Congress Cataloging-in-Publication Data
A catalog record for this book is available from the Library of Congress.

P 25 24 23 22 21 20 19 18 17 16 15 14 13 12 11 10 9 8 7 6 5 4 3 2 1

Y   34   33   32   31   30   29   28   27   26   25   24   23   22   21   20   19   18   17

To Bob
Your love has led me to God's grace.

Contents

Introduction

The Puzzle of Ourselves

Who in the world am I? Ah, that's the great puzzle.

ALICE IN WONDERLAND,
LEWIS CARROLL

I have always had a fondness for Alice. Not just because we share the same name. And not just because my favorite Halloween costume (age eight) was the Alice in Wonderland dress and apron that my mother made just for me. My adult fondness for Alice is because she asked the same question I ask: "Who in the world am I?" It is a question I have asked all of my life. It is an endless quest. As soon as I think I have discovered new things about myself, I have to ask, Who am I now that I think I know who I am?

THE PUZZLE

One of the most helpful tools for me in exploring this question is the Enneagram. The Enneagram is an ancient tool that can help us puzzle out who we are. As a child I looked to my friends to find out who I was. Like Alice I said, "I'm sure I'm not Ada. . . . I can't be Mabel. . . . Oh dear, how puzzling it all is!" As I grew into young adulthood, I looked to those whose faith I admired. But I never lived up to the standard I saw in their lives. Later in adulthood, I decided to set my own standards for the person I wanted to be. That didn't work either. The Enneagram led me to new discoveries about who I really am. Even more important, knowledge of the Enneagram has led me to the grace of God. I discovered through the Enneagram that I am not just my gifts, I am not just my failures, I am not just my compulsions. I am a person created by God, loved by God, and uniquely gifted to love others with God's merciful and gracious love.

Through the Enneagram God has taught me that I am not exactly who I think I am. I think I am what I do. I think I am an expression of my gifts. I think I know what life is about, that my values are all in place. But there is a part of me that is performing and pretending. And there is a vast part of who I am that remains untapped, unexplored, and unexpressed. Only God knows those parts of my being that I hide from others and from myself. The Enneagram itself does not make me a different person. But knowledge of the Enneagram does help me see who I truly am and offers me words to describe how I would like to be transformed by God's grace.

It has not been an easy journey. It is not a pleasant experience to embrace the discrepancy between who I am, who I want to be, who I think God wants me to be, and who others think I am. Like Alice, I sometimes feel as though I am falling down a rabbit hole. "Dear, dear! How queer everything is to-day! . . . I am so *very* tired of being all alone here!" And like the apostle Paul, sometimes I cry out, "I do not understand my own actions. For I do not do what I want, but I do the very thing I hate" (Romans 7:15 NRSV).

Paul's words reflect the experience of all human beings, whether they know it or not. We all struggle with the disparity between who we are and who we wish we were, between our inner lives and the lives we present to the outside world. Many people call this the difference between the true self and the false self. The Bible calls it the difference between the "old self" and the "new self" (Ephesians 4:22-24). As it describes the relationship between our gifts and our compulsions, the Enneagram gives words to help us describe the struggle we all share.

THE LOOKING GLASS HOUSE

In Lewis Carroll's sequel to *Alice in Wonderland,* Alice goes to the Looking Glass House. When she gets there, she discovers what we also know: when you peer into a looking glass, or a mirror, everything is backwards. When Alice picked up a book in the Looking Glass House, the words looked all wrong. Alice "puzzled over this for some time, but at last a bright thought struck her. 'Why, it's a Looking-Glass book, of course! And, if I hold it up to a glass, the words will all go the right way again.'" The Enneagram is like Alice's glass, or mirror. The Enneagram gives us a different view of ourselves, our gifts, our motivations, and our behavior. In the Looking Glass House where we live, we see ourselves quite backwards. When we hold ourselves up to the Enneagram, things "all go the right way again." The Enneagram helps us see ourselves as God sees us, not in the backwards way we see ourselves.

The Enneagram corrects the puzzling reflection we have of our own lives. We think we know our desires and motivations. And we think that our behavior comes from the best of our motivations. We think we are acting in love, but we see that we are really promoting ourselves and our own limited point of view. We believe we live in grace, but as we see ourselves in the paradigm of the Enneagram, we may see that even receiving grace has become something we feel we need to accomplish. We know God loves us unconditionally, but our false self tells us that pleasing God means that we have to do everything just right.

If we are honest with ourselves, we admit that what we think we believe does not always play out in our experiences and relationships. This is because we have so much backwards, but we don't know why. With Alice we say, "It's *rather* hard to understand!" With Paul we cry out, "I'm at the end of my rope. Is there no one who can do anything for me? Isn't that the real question?" (Romans 7:24 *The Message*).

The Enneagram helps us understand this dilemma. Through the Enneagram we learn that we do not have to strive to use our gifts beyond our capacity. We do not need to be like someone else, we do not need to have more abilities, and we do not need more opportunities to be the person God created us to be. In fact, life is not so much about being more as it is about letting go. (That is a puzzle indeed!) The Enneagram invites us to let go of our compulsions to express our giftedness, to let go of our need to love others according to our own standards, and to let go of our grasping for more, in order to come to God with empty hands, to receive the unique graces offered to us.

ENNEAGRAM PERSPECTIVES

There are many ways to look at the Enneagram. We need to know where we are going. Even Alice asked, "Would you tell me, please, which way I ought to go from here?"

"That depends a great deal," answered the Cheshire Cat, "on where you want to get to."

Alice replied, "I don't much care where."

"Then," said the Cat, "it doesn't much matter which way you go...."

"So long as I get somewhere."

"Oh," said the Cat, "you're sure to do that, if only you walk long enough."

Before we begin this long walk, let me say that "where I want to go" is to the grace of God. I come to the Enneagram as a Christian believer. Others approach the Enneagram from a variety of different perspectives. The Enneagram is only a tool. It is only words, as helpful as those are. I believe that by God's grace and help we will learn to live out the truths of these words in ways that reflect God's truth, the truth of Scripture, and the truth of our own lives. With this in mind I will include two important tools to take with you on this journey.

REFLECTION AND DISCUSSION QUESTIONS

The first tool is a set of questions to facilitate deeper personal reflection or group discussion about the chapter. One of the best ways to grow in the knowledge of the Enneagram is to experience it with other people, perhaps in a small group. This follows the oral tradition of the Enneagram. A woman who participated in a recent workshop had read extensively about the Enneagram. She told us that she hadn't really "gotten" it until the workshop, where she had the opportunity to hear many people talk about the Enneagram and to interact with others about its truths and applications to daily life.

As you engage with the Enneagram with others, remember that the Enneagram is a very personal experience. It can be encouraging, but it can also be embarrassing. As you discuss the ideas in this book, be respectful of each person in the group. Some will be introverts who will appreciate the conversation but may not speak up. Others will come with the pain of past relationships and circumstances. They may not be ready to share their own journey with others. And still others may be so new to the Enneagram and the spiritual journey that they can barely about talk about it.

But if the group is a safe place with a loving and welcoming atmosphere, it can be the best way to engage with the Enneagram.

Hopefully many in your group will be willing to talk about each part of the Enneagram and apply it honestly and authentically to their own lives. These questions are offered with that in mind. Use them as they suit your particular group. Take as long as you need with all of the questions you choose to discuss.

PERSONAL MEDITATIONS

At the end of each chapter I also include a personal meditation. The purpose of each meditation is not to teach more about the Enneagram but to invite you into deeper self-awareness. The idea is to invite you to be in God's presence, where transformation happens. The journey of the Enneagram, at its best, helps us to be open to the movements of God in our lives. Go slowly. Let your mind wander into the passage. Listen to what your heart, through the Holy Spirit, is saying to you.

If this reflective way to read the Bible is new for you, be patient with yourself. Remember that the Holy Spirit is guiding you. Often the first thing that comes to mind seems strange. *That can't be true!* you might think. But stay there and see what the Holy Spirit is whispering to you. Perhaps there is a truth you've missed or a misunderstanding the Spirit will correct. Listen carefully, and the Holy Spirit will guide you into truth and grace. (Chapter twelve gives a fuller description of reading Scripture in this way.)

▪ ▪ ▪

And so we begin! It may be a long walk, and we may fall down a few rabbit holes. It will not feel like Wonderland. But the journey will lead us to grace and truth. You will be invited to experience the life of Christ with new vigor, renewed commitment, and genuine faith. Come with me on this journey.

What Is the Enneagram, and Where Did It Come From?

The Enneagram captured me from the first workshop I attended in Madison, Wisconsin. I had my doubts that the mysterious circle with its numbers, lines, and arrows could tell me anything about myself. But as the presenter described each number, I began to see not only myself but also my husband, my daughters, even my neighbors. I saw why relationships get so confused. And I saw why I was often confused with myself. I saw a description of my spiritual journey that was unlike anything else I knew. I was hooked.

Several years later I attended another conference about the Enneagram that did not go as well for me. It was a two-day conference on the origins of the Enneagram. I did okay with the history. The presenters described the influence of various scholars and teachers on the Enneagram over the course of history. I learned about Evagrius Ponticus of the fifth century, Ramon Lull of the thirteenth century, and Oscar Ichazo, Claudio Naranjo, and Robert Ochs, all from the twentieth century. Not that I really knew who any of these people were, but at least I got the history part. Then the presenters moved on to the diagram of the Enneagram. I sat in the audience trying to listen well and nod wisely. But I had no idea what they were talking about. That was partly because I do not have the scientific or mathematical expertise that the presenters had. But I have since learned that I am not the only one confused.

THE ORIGINS OF THE ENNEAGRAM

As I have read more and more about the Enneagram, I have learned that its origins are clouded in mystery. One Enneagram book admits that "the exact origins of the Enneagram *symbol* have been lost to history; we do not know where it came from, any more than we know who discovered the wheel or how to write." Perhaps I was not so uninformed after all. We may never know the exact origins of the Enneagram or the Enneagram diagram.

We do know that the Christian roots of the Enneagram probably go back to the desert mothers and fathers of the fourth century. They are often considered the "spiritual directors" or mentors of the early church. As people sought them out for help on the spiritual journey, these teachers saw patterns of life that are reflected in the Enneagram. Since then the wisdom of the Enneagram has been passed down through oral tradition. This accounts for some of the confusion. Just as modern-day journalists give different reports about the same event, so historical and contemporary teachers of the Enneagram describe its history and content with a variety of words and perspectives.

In modern times this oral tradition has been passed down largely through the Catholic Church, but until the second half of the twentieth century the Enneagram was considered "secret knowledge." Laypeople, it was thought, could not handle this information with care and wisdom. When Richard Rohr, a Franciscan teacher of the Enneagram, learned of the Enneagram from his spiritual director in the 1970s, he was told not to pass it on in writing or to let anyone know where he got it. But, says Rohr, discovering the Enneagram was one of the "three great overwhelming spiritual experiences of my life. I could literally feel how something like scales fell from my eyes, and it became clear to me in a flash what I had previously been up to: I had always done the right thing . . . but for false motives." Breaking the silence, Rohr became a major influence in bringing the Enneagram to laypeople within the Catholic Church and, more recently, to Protestants. It took centuries, then, for the Enneagram to become accessible to someone like me.

THE ENNEAGRAM AS A SPIRITUAL JOURNEY

I wonder what the desert mothers and fathers of the fourth century would say about our understanding of the Enneagram today. Would they even recognize it after thousands of years of being passed down by oral tradition? Our current understanding of the Enneagram incorporates a variety of perspectives, different words, and different applications. The Enneagram is taught today from the vantage points of psychological understanding, the business world, and secular, nonreligious points of view.

My presentation of the Enneagram is from the perspective of a Christian's spiritual journey, looking at God's gifts to us, our failure to express these gifts in love, and God's gracious response to that failure. The Enneagram identifies the gifts we have been given. When we are freely and lovingly expressing these gifts, we are not held back by self-serving compulsive motivations. But on the journey of life, even when we want to live out of a truly loving place, we hit daily roadblocks. The Enneagram identifies the things we fixate on that cause us to get sidetracked or stuck on the journey. It shows where these fixations take us: right back into our compulsive, false-self perspective. In the words of the Enneagram, our compulsions are our "passions." Christians often call them sins. But from the Enneagram we learn that we are not left in our compulsions or sins. It also identifies the graces (or "virtues") given to us to lead us to transformation.

This is not a linear journey, from compulsion to transformation. It is more like a circle, or even a figure eight, that we weave in and out of many times a day. Richard Rohr said in one of his many talks on the Enneagram, "The agenda of the false self is to look good, to pretend. The biggest problem with the false self is not that it is there, but that we start to believe it ourselves. You can tell when the false self takes over because you become easily offended. The false self," he says, "is offended (about every three minutes) because it is fragile. The true self, on the other hand, is unoffendable." God invites us, through the wisdom of the Enneagram, to notice when we are acting out of false-self motivation. Then God, in love, invites us to let go of that motivation and return to living out of the gifts and grace given to us.

The Enneagram describes a life of growth, change, failure, and transformation. I have changed as I have traveled this Enneagram journey. By the grace of God, I am a different person today than I was when I went to that first workshop.

THE ENNEAGRAM DIAGRAM

Before we go further, let's take a look at the diagram of the Enneagram. The word *Enneagram* comes from the Greek words *ennea*, which means "nine," and *gram*, which means "point." The Enneagram suggests that there are nine vantage points from which humans view reality. These points are identified by numbers and are called spaces or types. The spaces are given different (yet similar) names by different Enneagram teachers. Figure 1 includes the names I will use in this book for each number.

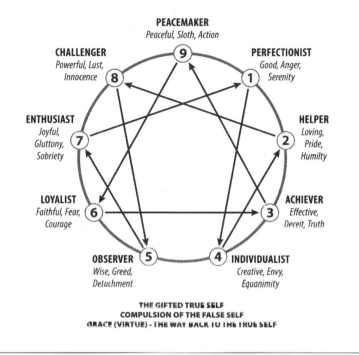

THE GIFTED TRUE SELF
COMPULSION OF THE FALSE SELF
GRACE (VIRTUE) - THE WAY BACK TO THE TRUE SELF

Figure 1. The nine spaces of the Enneagram

Underneath each name is a list identifying the main attribute of that person's true self, the compulsion of that person (in the false self), and the grace given to that person as an invitation to return to the true self. (Don't fall down the rabbit hole yet. I can explain all of this!)

Two other things to notice about this diagram: the lines with arrows pointing to and from each space and the numbers on both sides of each number, called "wings" in the language of the Enneagram. The arrows and the wings enhance the understanding of each space by suggesting what might happen under stress or at times of harmony in the life of each type. It's best to leave the arrows and wings in the background until the basics of the

Enneagram are embraced. We'll get to the wings and the arrows in chapter eight. First we need to look at a very brief summary of each Enneagram space. Then we will look at the concept of the true self and false self (chapter two) and at the triads of the Enneagram (chapter three). By that time we will be ready to look at the specifics of each Enneagram space (chapters four, five, and six) and at the application to our spiritual journeys.

THE THEORY OF THE ENNEAGRAM

As we begin, we will take a bird's-eye view of the Enneagram. Don't worry if this seems confusing at first. Human beings are confusing people. The Enneagram will eventually help sort that out.

The Enneagram suggests that we are all given particular gifts. Numbered one to nine, these gifts include goodness, love, effectiveness, creativity, wisdom, faithfulness, joy, power, and peace. We usually like our gifts. In fact, we like them so much, we become addicted to them. We cannot live a day without our giftedness being front and center in our lives. But as we try to do this, we find that we cannot express our gifts perfectly, others do not value our gifts as much as we think they should, and other people have different gifts that we may think look better or worse than our own gifts. When we become frustrated about these experiences with our gifts, it is as though we reach a roadblock on our daily spiritual journey. We try to circumvent the roadblock by exaggerating the gift we have been given. A person in the Three space, for instance, is often very successful and effective in what he does. This becomes so important that failure is totally unacceptable, something to be avoided at all costs. If failure cannot be avoided, the Three person unconsciously decides that a little deceit might cover it up. Or a person in the Eight space may be so enamored with her leadership and power that she tries to control everything and everyone. When this doesn't work, she doesn't know why and doubles down and tries harder to control, alienating her colleagues even more.

All of us live with some version of these examples. We all exaggerate what we value. We exaggerate the gift we have been given in order to try to look good, control life, and impress ourselves and others. When we do this, we are no longer free. We become compulsive about how we think we should express our gifts and how we think our gifts should be received. The Enneagram identifies the particular compulsions that accompany each gift.

The Enneagram does not leave us stuck in the mire of our compulsions. It suggests a grace to help us return to God's love, love for ourselves, and love for others. The classic presentation of the Enneagram uses the word *virtue* for this quality that helps us return to our true self. I prefer the word *grace*, a word used by many Enneagram presenters. This is a word that hints at something given to us freely, that we do not have to earn. For each of the nine spaces, a grace, or a perspective on life, is suggested to help loosen the grip of our compulsive thinking. The nine graces identified all hint at the mercy and love God offers all of us all of the time. As we receive the particular grace of our space, we also notice the graces of the other spaces and begin to participate in God's overwhelming mercy, indeed in God's grace. This will become clearer as we look at each space.

NINE PERSPECTIVES ON LIFE

The following summaries are very, very brief descriptions of each space. Think of these as a "Taste of the Enneagram." We have yet to get the full-course meal!

People in the *One space* are gifted with *goodness*. They do things well, very well. They are conscientious and ethical, striving for excellence. But on the journey of life, they discover that things are not always good, that they themselves are not always good. The false self convinces them that they are responsible for making life not only good but perfect. When things are not as perfect as they think they should be, Ones experience *anger*, toward themselves, situations, and others. God invites Ones to receive *serenity*, which is the ability to accept things as they are and to become less reactive when things are not perfect.

People in the *Two space* are especially gifted to *love*. But as Twos journey on in life, they discover that they actually like to feel needed by others even more than they like to love unselfishly. As they compulsively try to meet the needs of others, they deny their own needs and develop a *pride* that leads them to hover and control in the name of love. The false self convinces them that they know what everyone else needs but no one can know what they need. The grace that leads Twos back to the true self is *humility*. As they begin to acknowledge their own needs and weaknesses, God transforms them to be better able to love others with authenticity and grace.

People in the *Three space* are gifted to be *effective*, to succeed in making things happen. But as they succeed in life, Threes may become vain about their successes. When threatened with a sense of possible failure, Threes, in their false self, give in to *deceit*, the compulsion to twist the truth to fulfill the self-image they have created. *Truth* is the grace offered to Threes to experience God's transformation. The Enneagram reminds Threes to embrace and express truth about themselves, their abilities, their weakness, and emotions.

People in the *Four space* reflect the *creativity* of God. But because they cannot always make life and themselves creative and special, Fours give in to self-doubt, self-contempt, even self-hatred. This leads to *envy*, as they believe that everyone else has qualities they are missing. The grace offered to the Fours is *equanimity*, which gives balance to their emotions, allowing them to feel their feelings without getting stuck in them.

People in the *Five space* are gifted with *wisdom*. They are knowledgeable visionaries. But for Fives, the quest for knowledge and information is never ending. They become protective of their knowledge and may have an air of superiority. If they give in to the false self, they experience compulsive *avarice* or *greed*, taking in more and more knowledge but not wanting to give it out or let go of it. *Detachment* is the grace offered to Fives, allowing them to hold more loosely all that they know and move into their true self as they engage with others, even without knowing or understanding everything.

People in the *Six space* are *faithful*. They are loyal and easily influenced by authority. But they do not trust themselves. The false self says to Sixes that the opinion of others has more validity than their own ideas, and that they should embrace truth as others see it. Because they believe they must be prepared for every possible danger, their false self is especially prone to *fear*. God offers the grace of *courage* to Sixes. It takes courage for Sixes to learn to trust themselves and not assume that other perspectives have more validity than their own.

People in the *Seven space* are gifted with *joy*. But as they live with this gift, they are tempted to overstate the positive and to resist anything dark or negative. They protect themselves from the stresses of life by planning and dreaming. When the false self takes over, Sevens succumb to *gluttony*, wanting more and more of everything joyful or "happy," in order to avoid inner pain. The grace offered to Sevens is *sobriety*. This grace invites Sevens to take only what they need and live with that. In their true self, Sevens can enjoy life even if it includes some darkness.

People in the *Eight space* are often leaders. They are gifted with *power*. But Eights may deny their own vulnerability. To cope with this fear of weakness, they come to believe that they need to dominate others. "It's my way or the highway." The false self demands more and more power, giving in to *lust,* an insatiable passion for power over others. God invites Eights to receive the grace of *innocence,* a childlike capacity to admit weakness and vulnerability.

People in the *Nine space* are gifted with *peace.* They are calm and content and remind us that God is peaceful. But because they fear change and conflict, Nines may become indolent, not willing to exert themselves, even for things that are important. As the false self takes over, Nines can become *slothful* or *lazy.* This may lead them to become neglectful, taking the path of least resistance. God's grace to Nines is *action.* In their true self they are able to be more assertive, to state their own positions and preferences, and to become energized and involved in life.

SEEING THE ENNEAGRAM IN ORDINARY LIFE

Lest this all sound too simple, it is. Humanity is not neatly divided into nine categories. But the simplicity of the Enneagram is part of its genius. In the complexity of our life circumstances, our private motivations, and our inner inclinations, we lose sight of the unique ways we respond to life and we forget to appreciate that not everyone responds as we do. The Enneagram, quite simply, helps us see what we are doing.

Listen to how this might play out in an ordinary conversation when my husband and I connect in the late afternoon. If my husband asks me, "How was your day?" I would probably answer with a Four perspective, which can be a bit melancholic: "The committee chair didn't get back to me about the brochure. Now I'll be late with what they want me to do. The doctor never called about my test results. I don't think he likes me. I didn't have time to get the groceries so we have to eat leftovers." If I were a Seven, I might be more optimistic: "The committee chair didn't get back to me. Now I have extra time to work on the brochure. The doctor's office didn't call, so the test results must be okay. Oh, and I didn't get to the grocery store. Let's go out to eat." Or notice the underlying anger in how a One might respond: "The committee chair didn't call back. She should have! And I never heard from the doctor. We should switch to someone better. I should have gone to the grocery store, but lately they have so few cashiers, the lines are so long I didn't have time."

Each of us looks at life and relates to others within the perspective of our Enneagram space. Rohr often points out that "every viewpoint is a view from one point." But this does not mean that everyone in each space looks or sounds the same. Human beings are much too unique for that. Not all Fives value the same aspect of wisdom. Not all Eights want to be powerful in the same situations. And not all Twos want to help in the same ways. But the categories are still instructive. We observe categories in all of creation. Consider the variety of roses and the many types of maple trees. Not all roses are alike, and not all maple trees are alike. But if we did not have tree and flower categories and rose and maple categories, we would not do well tending the backyard. The Enneagram gives words to describe nine categories of human beings.

SPIRITUAL BLIND SPOTS

One reason the Enneagram confuses us at first is that it identifies our blind spots. We are, by definition, unaware of psychological and spiritual blind spots. I don't always know what I'm doing when I'm doing it. I can't see what's wrong with my compulsions. What's wrong with wanting to be an expert in using my gifts? The One person might think, unconsciously, *Why shouldn't I strive for perfection even though nothing is ever perfect?* Or the Nine might wonder, again unconsciously, *Why shouldn't I always be peaceful, even if I avoid conflict?* We all have times when we don't know why we are choosing to live life as we do, or we simply don't see what we are doing. Other people experience us differently from how we experience ourselves. Jesus asked, "Why do you see the speck that is in your brother's eye, but do not notice the log that is in your own eye?" (Matthew 7:3 RSV). Our blind spots are the logs in our eyes. The Enneagram is trying to point out to me things about myself I can't and don't want to see.

Our Enneagram compulsions are like rocks on a dark path. We stumble over them because we cannot see them. People in the Two space, for instance, stumble over their invasiveness and control as they compulsively try to help people. Those in the Six space stumble over their fear of disloyalty or disobedience as they give in to the compelling influence of authority figures in their lives.

The problem with our blind spots is not just that we are frustrated with life, others, and ourselves. Our blind spots are powerful deterrents to our spiritual growth. To the extent that we remain unaware of what is motivating us, we are not free. Learning about the Enneagram has helped me embrace the truth that God gave me gifts because God loves me and has equipped me to love others, not because my gifts are so impressive. God does not love me more because of my gifts. This truth has been immensely freeing for me. But it is counterintuitive and contrary to my normal thoughts and feelings.

MY NATIVE LANGUAGE

Jesus said that the enemy of our faith is the great deceiver. "When he lies," Jesus said, "he speaks his native language" (John 8:44). I have learned the language of the great deceiver well. In many ways it has become my native language. In order to grow spiritually, I need to translate my inner language into the language of God. Through the Enneagram I can see that my particular native language is the language of the Four. The lies I believe are second nature to me. Among other things, I believe that even though I am gifted in creativity, I must be extraordinarily special in all that I do. I believe that I am uniquely burdened by being sensitive and that others always have something I am missing. I did not even know I believed these lies until I learned I was a Four. In fact, when I first picked up a book about the Enneagram (to prepare for that first conference), I knew for sure that I was *not* a Four. That's how blind I was!

Looking beyond our blind spots to the truth of who we are is a difficult process. It is no surprise, then, that finding our "home space" can be a challenge. Chapter seven is devoted to practical ways we can meet this challenge and find the space that best describes our gifts as well as our compulsions.

SELF-AWARENESS

Learning the language of the Enneagram invites us into deeper self-awareness. *Who in the world am I?* This is not a narcissistic question. If I do not know who I am, I cannot see the log in my own eye, I do not know the full extent of God's grace, and I am trapped in ongoing patterns of living that are not life giving. As I have continued on in the journey of learning the truths of the Enneagram, I have become more and more grateful that the knowledge it gives increases my own self-awareness, even if at first I don't like what I see.

I am willing to journey on because this kind of awareness is essential to spiritual growth and intimacy with God. John Calvin wrote:

Nearly all wisdom we possess . . . consists of two parts: the knowledge of God and of ourselves. . . . The knowledge of ourselves not only arouses us to seek God, but also, as it were, leads us by the hand to find him.

David Benner wrote more recently:

Lack of awareness is the ground of our dis-ease and brokenness. . . . Choosing awareness opens up to finding God in the midst of our present realities. . . . Awareness is the key to so much. This is why it is, in my opinion, the single most important spiritual practice.

These are strong words from respected Christian leaders teaching hundreds of years apart. We would do well to listen. Our spiritual blind spots are not just a matter of stumbling and bruising the knees of our soul. Our blind spots keep us from knowing the love of God. If I am hiding behind a blind spot, I am unconsciously trying to keep God, others, and myself from the love that God offers. Knowledge of the Enneagram has led me into a self-awareness that has drawn me closer to the heart of God.

This book, then, is about much more than just the Enneagram. It is about the growth of inner self-awareness. It is about my relationship with my Creator, who loves parts of my being that I try to hide from others and from myself. This is a book about my experience of God's love and human love and my view of myself and of others. By God's grace, self-awareness doesn't happen quickly. (We couldn't handle that!) Slowly, slowly, the Spirit of God helps us see more and more of who we are and who we could be. The Enneagram is one tool to help us along this spiritual journey of awareness.

But this is not a journey to be made alone. I hope this book will be a companion for you as you engage with the Enneagram. I hope you will discuss the Enneagram with friends. And I hope you will pray about what you are learning from the Enneagram. May God guide you to truth, which, by grace, will set you free.

FOR REFLECTION AND DISCUSSION

1. Where did you first hear about the Enneagram?

2. "The Enneagram suggests that we are all given particular gifts. Numbered one to nine, these gifts include goodness, love, effectiveness, creativity, wisdom, faithfulness, joy, power, and peace." Which of these gifts do you think you have? Which ones would you like to have?

3. "We cannot live a day without our giftedness being front and center in our lives. But as we try to do this, we find that we cannot express our gifts perfectly, others do not value our gifts as much as we think they should, and other people have different gifts that we may think look better or worse than our own gifts. When we become frustrated about these experiences with our gifts, it is as though we reach a roadblock in our daily spiritual journey. We try to circumvent the roadblock by exaggerating the gift we have been given." How do you think each of these gifts might look when it is exaggerated? Can you think of a time when you have exaggerated your own gifts?

4. As you look over the descriptions of each space, which one do you think you might identify with the most? In what ways do you relate to that space?

5. "One reason the Enneagram confuses us at first is that it identifies our blind spots." What is a psychological or spiritual blind spot? When have you discovered one of your own blind spots? How do you think the Enneagram reveals our blind spots?

A Personal Meditation
The Rich Young Ruler: Mark 10:17-21

As Jesus started on his way, a man ran up to him and fell on his knees before him. "Good teacher," he asked, "what must I do to inherit eternal life?"

"Why do you call me good?" Jesus answered. "No one is good—except God alone. You know the commandments: 'You shall not murder, you shall not commit adultery, you shall not steal, you shall not give false testimony, you shall not defraud, honor your father and mother.'"

"Teacher," he declared, "all these I have kept since I was a boy."

Jesus looked at him and loved him. "One thing you lack," he said. "Go, sell everything you have and give to the poor, and you will have treasure in heaven. Then come, follow me."

---

1. What do you think this young man might have been feeling as he ran up to Jesus? If you did that, what do you think you would be feeling?

2. What is the first question you would ask Jesus today? How do you think Jesus might answer you? Notice how you might respond to the answer Jesus gives you.

3. "Jesus looked at him and loved him." Spend some time with this image. Can you think of someone who has looked at you with love? What was that like? If you can't think of anyone, tell God about how you feel about what you've missed. Spend a few minutes imagining Jesus looking at you and loving you.

4. Take some time to muse about how being loved frees you to be self-aware. What have you learned so far about yourself from the Enneagram that you would like to bring into the experience of God's love?

The True Self
and the False Self

My friend Sheila is retired from a lifetime in Christian ministry, but she continues to use her gifts of hospitality for the benefit of friends and family. When she invited me to lunch along with several others, I was eager to accept the invitation—with one slight caveat: Could I bring along a few questions about the Enneagram? My friends know that when I am deeply involved in a writing project, I am prone to talk about it all the time. So with Sheila's permission I arrived armed with questions I wanted to ask about the true self and the false self, a concept I will explore in this chapter. I did wait until we had lunch on our plates, but then I jumped in. I described a bit about what I meant by the terms *false self* and *true self*, and then I asked, "How do you experience the true self and the false self in ordinary life?"

Sheila spoke up right away, telling us about her frustrations with herself and the meal in front of us. First of all, she said, she was embarrassed about the holes in the wall where a curtain rod had been replaced. (I hadn't noticed.) The dishes on the table were not her favorite because in a moment of generosity she had given away the other ones. (The ones on the table were beautiful.) The fruit salad didn't have the right dressing. (It was delicious.) The only thing my friend felt good about was the quiche. (Someone else had made it.)

Sheila struggled with this not because she is depressed or self-deprecating. She struggled because she is very honest and very self-aware. She knew that as she prepared for us to come to lunch, she was facing her false self head-on. For her, the false self takes on the persona of an inner critic, reminding her that nothing she does meets her own standards of perfection. Her inner critic has been part of her life for a long, long time. She recognized the characteristics of the false self from her years in ministry as well as from her experiences in marriage and parenting. Now, she discovered, her false self had retired with her.

Sheila's false self wants to be perfect. This reflects Sheila's space on the Enneagram, but the false self crosses over all the Enneagram spaces. The false self wants to impress people. The false self has expectations that can never be met. The false self drains us of joy. Sheila said that what she really wanted was that we feel loved as we shared the meal together, but her false self challenged every attempt she made to express love.

What Sheila didn't know was that I experienced love from the moment I walked in her front door. I immediately saw the pots of flowers on her deck and smelled the wonderful aroma of lunch. Then I noticed the dining room table—more flowers, beautiful place settings, and yummy food. I could tell she had put time, thought, and love into preparing for our arrival. I felt loved.

The love I received from Sheila was the love of God. We know from the Bible that God is love (1 John 4:16). Created in the image of God, we are, in our essence, love. But the standards and lies of the false self had robbed Sheila of the pleasure of knowing that her love had embraced us all in spite of the things she thought were not perfect. Different people experience the false self in slightly different ways. Someone else might have invited us to lunch (or planned a business meeting) while thinking compulsively about how she could control the conversation. Another person might have struggled with wanting everything to be peaceful, worrying about how to make sure there was no conflict. Or still another person may have spent more time thinking about the topics she would bring up for discussion and how she could look wise and knowledgeable in the conversation. The Enneagram helps us give names to the ways the false self tempts us.

The false self is the person we think we should be but are not. It is the person we want others to think we are. The false self perpetuates the illusion that we are able to love perfectly, to be wise and all-knowing, and to be in control of life. The false self thrives on success and achievement. The problem is not that the false self is a bad person. The problem is that the false self is a façade. It is an imitation of God that we use to impress others. The false self languishes in pretense and in grasping for abilities and gifts that are not ours to have. The true self, on the other hand, truly expresses the gifts God has given us to love well.

NEW WORDS FOR OLD TRUTHS

The terms *false self* and *true self* are contemporary terms for deep truths. The apostle Paul spoke of the "old self" (Romans 6:6). We might also say the "ego self." To the false-old-ego self, life is all about me. The false self needs constant approval. It is competitive and defensive. The false self wants to achieve rather than receive. It behaves in ways we think guarantee us to be accepted, needed, and admired. Living in this place is exhausting. But the temptation to hang on to the false self is a 24/7 experience.

In contrast, God invites us to be the person created in the image of divine love, instinctively and probably unconsciously reflecting the love of God. This is the new self (2 Corinthians 5:17), a unique person who has been given characteristics, desires, and gifts that reflect who God is. Our true self includes the gifts we were given when we were created but without the tainting of our self-serving pride. According to the New Testament the new/true self is free (2 Corinthians 3:17), lives as Jesus lived in truth and grace (John 1:14), and manifests the fruits of the Holy Spirit (Galatians 5:22-23). The true self is focused, not fragmented by the illusions of the false self. The true self recognizes personal limitations as well as God's invitation to love others out of the gifts given to us. The true self knows it is not in charge of its own life, let alone of the world. In short, the true self is God-centered rather than ego-centered.

Briefly stated, using new and old words, the false self is the self-centered self, the ego self, the old self, the competitive self, the well-defended self, and, ultimately, the self that deceives us and the world. But do not make the mistake of identifying the behaviors and activities of the false self as "sins." We know from the Enneagram that the false self values good behavior: goodness, loving deeds, getting things done, creativity, wise ideas, obedience, a joyful perspective, leadership, and peacefulness.

The lure of the false self reminds me of what happened to my daughter in the grocery store. Elisa still remembers a terrifying moment in the produce section. She was young, too young for school but old enough to be walking the aisles of the grocery store with Mommy. Somewhere between the lettuce and the grapefruit, she let go of my hand and wandered a few feet away. Ready to return to the security of my presence she reached up to take my hand, but—horrors! That was *not* Mommy up there.

She had taken the wrong hand. The hand she grabbed did not belong to a bad person. In all probability, it belonged to another mommy. But it was not *her* mommy's hand. She let go quickly and looked around for the right mommy. There I was, checking out the apples. Running over to me, she grabbed my leg, at home again where she was loved and protected.

As grownups we sometimes do the same thing spiritually that Elisa did physically as a child. We walk away, just a bit, from the God who loves us, and then when we need comfort, we reach up and take the wrong hand. The hand we take does not belong to a bad person. This person looks like someone who loves us and will protect us. We think we can hang on to this hand and everything will be all right. But eventually we start to panic, realizing that the hand we are holding does not belong to someone who can give life. The hand we are holding belongs to our false self.

The problem is that for each of us, the false self looks like someone who can help us. After all, expressing our gifts is a good thing. But when I grab the hand of my false self, I begin to do good things for the wrong reasons. The false self wants the credit and recognition. The true self, on the other hand, is the redeemed self, the new self, the soul self, the loving self, the humble self, the open self, and the authentic self. The true self does not need the credit.

Jesus might say to the false self what he said to Martha: "You are worried and upset about many things, but few things are needed—or indeed only one" (Luke 10:41-42). The false self is worried and upset about how it behaves, what it thinks, and what others think. The true self holds the outcome of its gifted behavior loosely, willing to be recognized or not. The true self recognizes that our gifts come from God and not from our own efforts. The false self says, "My kingdom come." The true self says, "Thy kingdom come."

Unlike my daughter's momentary panic at reaching for the wrong hand, we grab the wrong hand of the false self many times a day. We grab the wrong hand in the office as well as at the grocery store, at home as well as in church, in public as well as in private. The false self reaches out to us, offering a hand even when we don't ask. The false self promises us false comfort, false help, and false compliments. And unlike my daughter, we may not even notice that we have grabbed the wrong hand. The false self is hidden from our vision by pride, denial, and illusion. The masquerade of the false self works on us as well as others.

THE DISGUISES OF THE FALSE SELF

"Satan himself masquerades as an angel of light," according to the apostle Paul in his letter to the early church at Corinth (2 Corinthians 11:14). The false self has endless masks and disguises, and they all look pretty good. Like my granddaughters' overflowing bin of dress-up clothes, there is something for every occasion. "What dress-up outfit would I like for today? Oh, dear. That one is ripped. Never mind, there are more in the bin." The Enneagram does not describe all of the options for our false-self disguises. But it does identify our favorites. Before we look at the favorite false-self disguises for each space, we need to look at the wide range of choices. What are the common characteristics we are most likely to see in the false self?

At the core of the false self is *pride*. The false self wants to impress others. The false self wants to be right, to be perfect, to be admired. The false self is fearful and defensive. The false self is self-promoting and wants to be in control. Dr. David Benner says that

> at the core of the false self is a desire to preserve an image of our self and a way of relating to the world. This is our personal style—how we think of ourselves and how we want others to see us and think of us. . . . The false self is like the air we breathe. We have become so accustomed to its presence that we are no longer aware of it.

This is a little discouraging. If the false self is like the air I breathe, how will I know when I am breathing in the false self? If the false self wears a disguise, how will I recognize it? Thankfully, there are hints we can notice when we are breathing in the stale air of the false self. Here is a CliffsNotes list of things we might notice in our own lives when we are living in the false self.

We think we should be in control of our lives and our worlds.

We think we are entitled to have our goals and desires met.

We deny our own limitations and foibles.

We overtly or covertly look for appreciation, recognition, or even fame.

We feel misunderstood and alienated from others.

We want to know and explain everything.

We want to be independent and not needy.

We are defensive, protecting the image of ourselves we want to have.

We often live in the past or the future rather than accepting the present reality.

LIVING OUT OF THE TRUE SELF

A corresponding list for the true self looks quite different. This is not a list of qualities we should compulsively try to achieve. (That's the false self talking.) Rather, we can notice when we see these things in our life and celebrate the grace of God as transformation to the true self gradually happens.

We live freely, limited only by God's love.

We occasionally, consciously, let go of our desire for control.

We learn to distinguish between the voice of our ego and the voice of God's love.

We allow others to disagree with us without responding with anger or shame.

We feel focused more often than fragmented.

We resist letting our desire for security have too much influence in our decisions.

We become more aware of when we are reacting to life rather than receiving life.

We believe that God is loving us in the present moment, whatever it holds.

We notice with surprise that the fruits of the Holy Spirit are evident in our lives.

People often notice that they can't see the true self in day-to-day life. We might recognize it with hindsight, but on an ordinary day the true self is almost invisible to us. We are, according to Paul, the "aroma" of Christ (2 Corinthians 2:15). And as we know from unpleasant experience, people cannot smell their own aroma! So we live by faith that God is living through us, expressing love in our true selves. Even if we can't see that, or smell the aroma, it is still there.

LETTING GO OF THE FALSE SELF

The good news about the false self is that by grace we can learn to gradually let go of its influence. We do not need to throw a temper tantrum that we have gone in the wrong direction. We can look up and see the merciful, loving God looking for us. God's intention is that we live in love. When asked what was the most important commandment, Jesus replied, "Love the Lord your God with all your heart and with all your soul and with all your mind.' This is the first and greatest commandment. And the second is like it: 'Love your neighbor as yourself.' All the Law and the Prophets hang on these two commandments" (Matthew 22:37-40). So everything in the Old and New Testaments revolves around loving God, loving others, and loving ourselves. The false self does not believe that. We know these truths, but we forget them. And into that forgetful void, the false self reaches for our hand. It is a transforming experience to remember God's love again and to let go of the demand and expectations of the false self. Knowledge of the Enneagram helps us do that.

The Enneagram shows us that the false self is hiding in plain sight—in the way we express our gifts. The false self masquerades as the perfect, exaggerated expression of our giftedness. When we are threatened, offended, or under stress, we rev up our gifts, compulsively trying to convince others (and ourselves) that we are worthy to be admired because we are so very gifted. Or we try to protect ourselves from our fears by overplaying what we do well. When all else fails, we grab on and try to control life with the very gifts God gave us to help us love others.

The Enneagram helps take off our false-self masks by telling us truth. We are not our gifts. We are beloved children of God. We do not have to have all the gifts of God in order to reflect the image of God. By God's grace, the gifts we have reflect more of God's love than we can imagine. And we do not need to compulsively make our gifts front and center in our lives. Just as we have freely received our gifts, we are invited to freely receive the opportunity to give them to others.

This perspective sounds like a foreign language to the false self. We are always needing to translate from our native false-self language to the language of the Creator God. Learning about the Enneagram helps us do that by giving us a language that describes both the true self and the false self. But the Enneagram tells it "slant." The poet Emily Dickinson reminds us, "Tell all the truth, but tell it slant. . . . The truth must dazzle gradually / Or every man be blind." The Enneagram does not dazzle us with the truth but invites us to plumb the depths of its multilayered diagram. As we do this, we also plumb the depths of ourselves and begin to understand ourselves in new ways as the truth "slants" toward us. Slowly, slowly, we see the light of the true self and begin to let go of the façade of the false self.

We learn to look behind the behaviors of the various Enneagram spaces to the motivation. The false self usually behaves very well. But the motivation behind the behavior is not so pretty. We do not want to admit that our motivation may not correspond with the appearance of our behavior. The Enneagram should make us so uncomfortable with this discrepancy that we long for change and growth. Many people say that if you really like your Enneagram space, you probably haven't found it yet. Uncovering our motivation can be painful. T. S. Eliot wrote in the "The Four Quartets" that "human kind cannot bear very much reality." We need to move cautiously and carefully as we uncover the false self. We need all the help we can get.

THE JOURNEY OF THE TRUE SELF

The place where we begin is a willingness to become self-aware, to be honest with ourselves. Only when we have the courage to notice the hints that we are living out of our false self can we begin the journey to the true self. The Enneagram invites us to do that. My friend Sheila told us that the day before we came for lunch, she caught herself listening to her false self when she thought twice about spending way too much money to get exactly the right ingredients for the salad dressing. Standing in the grocery aisle, she had a wake-up call and was able to stop the downward spiral into her false-self thinking and embrace again the values of her true self.

Knowing the typical characteristics of our Enneagram space allows us to catch ourselves in the act. We can silently whisper "Help!" to the God of grace. It is best not to attack the false self. ("Stop thinking like that! That's bad/wrong/sinful!") That only gives the false self more power. We cannot "manage" the false self because it will find another way to get to us. We can only acknowledge that we want to let go. Being aware of what is happening and acknowledging a desire to disbelieve the false-self illusions is the place we need to start.

It helps when we can notice the times we are most vulnerable to the false self. For me, this is often when I am tired. For others it may be when they are in charge of something or wishing they were in charge. For someone else it might be when speaking to an adoring audience, receiving admiration, or being asked to take on an impressive project. Still others notice the false self showing up when they are discouraged by the overwhelming events of life.

Acknowledging our times of vulnerability helps us not to be totally blindsided by the false self. And, strangely enough, as we accept the presence and the weaknesses of the false self, we begin to grow into the true self. This sounds crazy to me since I spend so much time just hoping my false self will disappear. But Judith Hougen says that self-acceptance is the hallmark of the true self:

> Self-acceptance gives assent to be who I am—a small, limited person with bents toward sin as well as hungers for holiness—and allows me to live with all my contradictions, because my will, at least on good days is to "walk in the light, as he is in the light."

If I can catch myself in the act, notice, and accept myself, then perhaps I will move toward transformation. But the journey from the false self to the true self is circuitous and lifelong. I wish I could say there are handy MapQuest directions. ("In current traffic, this journey takes seventeen minutes.") But the journey is more like those offered by antique maps. Just as these maps were incomplete and often wrong, so the maps of our false self are incomplete and usually wrong. Even the maps of our true self are sometimes confusing. But even with inaccurate maps, Columbus reached America.

In a similar way, our stumbling attempts to move into the true self will lead us to discoveries of God's grace. No human map is perfect. God's ways are too mysterious for that. We will always be learning new ways to walk in truth and grace. But the Enneagram is a good map as we continue on the journey. Knowledge of the Enneagram helps us identify the gifts of our true self as well as the cliffs where we might fall off into the false self. As we become more self-aware, we become more loving people.

FOR REFLECTION AND DISCUSSION

1. "The false self is the person we think we should be but are not. . . . The problem is not that the false self is a bad person. The problem is that the false self is a façade. It is an imitation of God that we use to impress others." How would you define *false self* in your own words? What difference does it make if we choose to live out of our false self?

2. The true self is "a unique person who has been given characteristics, desires, and gifts that reflect who God is. . . . The true self recognizes personal limitations as well as God's invitation to love others out of the gifts given to us. The true self knows it is not in charge of its own life, let alone of the world. In short, the true self is God-centered rather than ego-centered." What experiences of the true self have you had in your own life or in relating to someone else?

   What do you notice about the differences between living out of the false self and living out of the true self?

3. Which of the characteristics of the false self do you see expressed most often in your own world?

   Which are most tempting to you personally?

   When are you most likely to act out of your false self?

4. Which of the characteristics of the true self do you see most often in your own world?

Which ones would you most like to see in your own life?

What helps you the most to act out of your true self?

5. "The place where we begin is a willingness to become self-aware, to be honest with ourselves. Only when we have the courage to notice the hints that we are living out of our false self can we begin the journey to the true self." What is your opinion about the value of being "self-aware"?

What fears do you have about being more self-aware?

How do you think self-awareness helps us on our spiritual journey?

A Personal Meditation
Jesus' View of Life: Matthew 6:31-34

[Jesus said,] "What I'm trying to do here is to get you to relax, to not be so preoccupied with getting, so you can respond to God's giving. People who don't know God and the way he works fuss over these things, but you know both God and how he works. Steep your life in God-reality, God-initiative, God-provisions. Don't worry about missing out. You'll find all your everyday human concerns will be met.

"Give your entire attention to what God is doing right now, and don't get worked up about what may or may not happen tomorrow. God will help you deal with whatever hard things come up when the time comes." (The Message)

1. Read Jesus' words slowly, at least twice, perhaps once out loud.

2. Notice one word or phrase the catches your attention.

3. How does that word or phrase apply to your life today? Is there any insight from your knowledge of the Enneagram that helps you see why the Holy Spirit is drawing you to this word or phrase?

4. How does this word or phrase reflect what you have learned about your true self and your false self?

A spiritual practice: Write your word or phrase on a 3 x 5 card and repeat it to yourself ten times each day for two weeks. As you repeat the word, whether or not you think about it or even pray about it, God will plant it in your heart and give it life in your soul.

3

The Triads of the Enneagram

The weather in Chicago is known to be very cold in the winter and very hot in the summer. One blistering day last summer I saw my neighbor in the driveway. Trying to be friendly, I waved and offered a generic weather-related greeting. "Hi, there. It sure is hot today, isn't it?" She wasn't buying that. "I don't think so. I'm freezing. I just came from the office. It was way too cold in there." Oops. How could I respond to that? I certainly didn't want to argue about the weather, but I felt rebuffed. Good thing I knew about the Enneagram. As insignificant as the interchange was, I knew it was an Enneagram moment. My neighbor and I are clearly in different triads in the Enneagram paradigm.

THE TRIADS

A good place to begin learning about the Enneagram is with the triads. The nine spaces of the Enneagram are divided into three parts: the heart triad (2, 3, 4), the head triad (5, 6, 7), and the gut triad (8, 9, 1). The three spaces in each triad have similar characteristics, but each space expresses those similarities in slightly different ways. Those in the heart triad live life based on feeling. Those in the head triad live life based on thinking. And those in the gut triad respond to life with their gut instinct. The triads are a good place to start because at first blush it is often easier to identify your triad than your specific space. If you can identify your triad, then you've narrowed down your space possibilities to three.

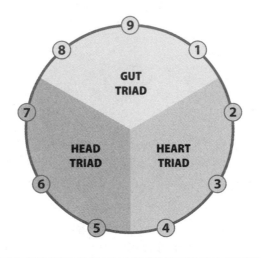

Figure 2. The triads

The Enneagram, with its triads and spaces, is descriptive, not prescriptive. It makes observations about people in different categories. But it would be a mistake to assume that we can predict how people in each triad or space will respond to life. Categories are just that—groupings of people and things with similarities but also differences. Not all flowers are the same. Marigolds and impatiens need water and sunlight, but in different amounts. All athletes are competitive, but not all athletes have the same skills sets. Even though the Enneagram sees human beings in nine categories, we know that all people are infinitely unique. So we dare not look at the Enneagram to *predict* human behavior, let alone motivation.

The gift of the Enneagram is in the way it describes our similarities as well as our differences.

For each triad I will describe the true self, the roadblocks for those in this triad, the false self as it is manifested in the triad, and the road home, back to the true self. Remember, the true self reflects the God of love and grace. The false self is the ego-driven self, out to serve our particular compulsions. We take the road from the true self to the false self and back to the true self many times a day.

THE HEART TRIAD (2, 3, 4)

When they are living out of the true self, people in the heart triad have strong relational energy. It is as though they have a magnetic attraction to other people and relationships. They may be introverted temperamentally in terms of where they get their energy (from being alone), but relationally they are naturally social. They are usually helpful. They are frequently very effective and successful. And they often have a creative bent. They adapt to what they think others want of them. Their attention goes into making connections.

People in this triad hit roadblocks in life and on their spiritual journey when they begin to feel responsible for the world around them. They feel responsible not only for their own foibles but for the problems of others. This fixation plunges them into anxiety and busyness.

Anxious busyness can be productive or unproductive. I am reminded of a time I dropped my teenage daughters off at high school. We had left the house angry and upset. I don't remember the particular issue du jour, but I do remember my own frustrations. I couldn't help them. I couldn't fix their problems. I was a failure as a parent. Complicating things more, I was mad at them for having the problems in the first place. And I was mad at myself for being mad at them. Unwittingly translating that into the anxious busyness of someone in the heart triad, I left them at school, went home, and scrubbed the bathtub to a shining glory. I didn't know at the time that this was another Enneagram moment, but I did get a clean bathtub.

Because they feel responsible for *everything*, people in the heart triad try to fix everything. Anxiety leads them to activity. To others this may look like control or drivenness. But to those in the heart triad it is just being responsible.

But they cannot fix every problem, so people in this triad live with a sense of inadequacy and incompetency. They are forever comparing themselves with others. Usually they do not fare well in the comparison.

Do not be misled by the name of this triad. Yes, heart triad people feel deeply. But more often than not, they are unaware of their own feelings. They are probably more aware of others' feelings than their own. This tendency starts early. My beloved dog ate all my candy the year I dressed up as Alice in Wonderland for Halloween. As I looked at my dog with her tail between her legs in shame, I was much more concerned about her and how badly she felt than about my own sadness over losing my candy. This doesn't seem like a big deal now, but I continued the same pattern of ignoring my own feelings into my teenage years. This led to depression that lasted well into adulthood. I had taught myself not to listen to my own heart. Seeing this characteristic in the heart triad of the Enneagram helps me understand what I am doing. I no longer struggle with depression, but I still have to remind myself to pay attention to my own heart and feelings.

When the false self takes over for people in the heart triad, image becomes all important. What will people think of me? How do I compare to others? (If I fall short, I feel inadequate. If I come out on top, I feel guilty for causing others to feel inadequate.) All of this leads to shame, the conscious or unconscious feeling that plagues those in the heart triad. When they live in the false self, heart triad people try desperately to win the love of others. Their own needs and desires are muted. They pretend things are okay when they are not.

As depressing as this sounds (at least to someone in this triad), the Enneagram suggests a way out. When people in the heart triad open themselves to transformation, they admit that they cannot fix the problems of humanity. They take notice of themselves in the present moment. Suzanne Zuercher in *Enneagram Spirituality* says that the present moment for Twos, Threes, and Fours is only a crack that separates the past from the future. Heart triad people ruminate about the past and what they did wrong, or plan for the future and how they can impress people. The present? Well, that will pass.

God invites people in this triad to begin to look within and let go of the grip that the needs and opinions of others have on them. This is one of the reasons why daily times of quiet and reflection are so important for people in this triad. By setting aside time to intentionally be alone, away from the pull of other people on their lives, heart triad people can be present to themselves and are then able to be present to those they love.

The disguises of the false self for those in the heart triad are manifold. When they are living in their false selves, people in the heart triad believe that people will like them if they can somehow manage not to offend anyone. So they try to portray a very accepting, very agreeable image. Sometimes this even seems ingratiating. And it is exhausting. To do this, they teach themselves to resist their own needs. To live with this disguise, heart triad people sacrifice their own feelings for the sake of identifying with others' feelings. They may also sacrifice reality for harmony if reality means that their feelings contradict someone else's perspective. The false self tells people in this triad that to prove their self-worth, they must put the problems of those they love (or those they want to impress) ahead of their own needs. It is a heavy burden to carry.

Shame has a way of attaching itself to the false self of the heart triad because people in this triad usually feel inadequate to meet the needs and expectations they think they are hearing from those around them. They are ashamed of this inadequacy.

People in the heart triad may be drawn in by the words of Jesus: "If you're content to be simply yourself, you will become more than yourself" (Luke 18:14 *The Message*). At first this probably sounds like a strange invitation to those in this triad. But as they embrace the truth of Jesus' words, they discover that by accepting themselves and letting go of trying to impress others, they actually become more loving people, living out of their true selves. They release the grip that the opinion of others has on them. They let go of having to fix all the problems of the world. They begin to experience humility, truth, and equanimity.

THE HEAD TRIAD (5, 6, 7)

People in the head triad experience life very differently from those in the heart triad. When living in the true self, people in the head triad observe life in order to take in information, put it in order, and imagine possibilities. For them, what is real is within their minds. They would agree with Descartes, the French philosopher of the seventeenth century, "I think, therefore I am." My husband, a card-carrying head triad person, says he lives life through his thoughts. When he travels, he packs his books and papers before his clothes. The wonderful thing about people in the head triad is that when they take action in the outer world, they offer new ways to see life, fitting pieces together in a way others cannot.

People in the head triad meet roadblocks in their journey when they keep collecting more and more information and allow fear to keep them from acting on their information. They look for safety by continually putting their inner world in order. Even though they may speak of action in the future, it is hard for them to move there.

Because their inner world is so important and receives so much attention, they often feel isolated from others, but they resent losing privacy and independence when others start paying attention to them. Fear may also lead them to hope that someone else will confirm or act on the insights they bring to the table.

When the roadblocks become overwhelming, the false self rushes in. This leads to emotional paralysis for the people in the head triad. They retreat into their mental strategies. For some in the head triad, this means collecting endless information. Others collect guidelines and rules to tell them what to do, while others collect experiences. Introverted head triad people may simply move away from others and retreat to their own minds. Extroverted head triad people often try to collect events and conversations, but they may resist heartfelt conversations with others. For this reason, head triad people may feel forgotten and overlooked. This leads them to grasp at life. People in this triad can become legalistic, possessive, or gluttonous when the false self takes over.

Head triad people may hesitate to take meaningful action. When large personal decisions must be made, people in this triad think and think and think, often much longer than others think they need to. I often say that it is only by God's grace that my husband finally asked me to marry him. It took him a very long time to collect and organize the information he thought he needed about what it would be like to be married to me. I'm quite sure our marriage turned out differently from what he expected, even with all of his thinking!

For people in the head triad, the false self disguises itself as someone safe from all they fear. When living in their false self, people in the head triad believe that if their thinking is in order they will be protected from hidden danger. The false self for people in this triad is very busy organizing their inner world. When they do that well, by their own standards, the false self feels safe. This attachment to what is going on in the head is a heavy burden to bear. If another, perhaps contradictory, idea comes down the pike, those in this triad feel threatened that the new ideas will crash into the safe place they have created.

What the false self does not want to admit is that this safety is an illusion. And this illusion keeps people in this triad from turning their ideas into actions. If my mind is in order, if my thinking is right, if I am obeying all the rules, what more do you want me to do? The false self may become paralyzed as it focuses on strategies, beliefs, and plans. Fear attaches itself to the false self of those in the head triad. In this fear, they may become possessive about their own agendas, legalistic about the rules all around them, or gluttonous about the experiences they long for.

As people in this triad move away from the false self to the true self, they begin to move outside of themselves and learn to engage more freely with other people. They become less compulsive about ordering their inner world and more willing to risk not knowing or understanding everything. They let go of their attachment to their thoughts and ideas and have the courage to embrace life rather than fear it.

When people in the head triad open to God's transformation they begin to realize they do not need to understand life in order to live it. They are invited by God's Spirit to move outside of their heads and to be engaged and energized by other people. This frees them to risk sharing their inner world and their feelings with others and with God. Now that my husband knows this about himself and takes greater risks in sharing his feelings with me, I can hear his feelings directly from him. That's helpful to both of us because it keeps me from imagining (in my heart triad tendency) what he is feeling, which may or may not be accurate.

People in the head triad often find that their spiritual journey is enriched by moving outside of themselves. Being in nature is one way of moving outside, literally and emotionally. Sitting outside, going on a hike, or even playing a round of golf can be good for head triad people.

As transformation takes place, head triad people begin to take action, even before they understand or have collected as much information as they would like. They will always be most at home within themselves, but moving out of their minds into action becomes less threatening as they experience the grace of transformation. "Faith," the author of Hebrews says, "is confidence in what we hope for and assurance about what we do not see" (Hebrews 11:1). This is a challenge and an invitation to those in the head triad, but it is this faith in truths beyond what they can see and what they can know with their minds that helps head triad people detach from their own understanding and find the courage and sobriety they long for.

THE GUT TRIAD (8, 9, 1)

When people in the gut triad are living out of the true self, they are strong, opinionated, and people of high moral standards. They are often leaders. They challenge systems that they see as ineffective, harmful, or unjust.

Unlike people in the heart triad who barely notice the present moment, or people in the head triad who spend a lot of time planning the future, people in the gut triad respond deeply and totally to what is happening now. From this stance, they instinctively "dig in" rather than give in to others or to circumstances. And unlike people in the heart triad or the head triad, people in this triad are comfortable and energized by both their inner and their outer worlds. They are decisive and speak with conviction. They see life as a battle to be won and offer their services in leading the charge.

Since not everyone else likes to be led into battle, people in the gut triad often meet resistance in their efforts to control other people and circumstances. This leads them to a roadblock of anger. In fact, they convert many of their emotions into anger. They often feel like they are drowning in emotional intensity. They try to control this intensity with reason and logic. Others may think their logic is cold hearted. Think of the parent who responds to a child's fears with the comment, "You're just going to have to get over that." The parent is only telling the child what he tells himself all the time when he feels fearful or weak.

Richard Rohr, a gut person himself, is quick to point out that gut people store their judgment in the body. Their right-versus-wrong responses to life cause shock waves to go through their bodies, "like full body blows," says Rohr.

Gut triad people do not like weakness or vulnerability. In the qualifying program I attended for the Enneagram, one of my fellow students was a woman who owned a trucking company. Covered with tattoos, her whole being emitted the strength of someone in the gut triad. The instructor put a list on the board of the qualities an Eight does not like, including weakness, un-fairness, being a wimp, and dependency. The trucking company owner put out her hand, turned away, and almost shouted, "Oh I *hate* those things!" Her response would be typical of many in the gut triad.

When the false self takes over for those in this triad, they simply cannot not win. Their very survival depends on being in charge, not being vulnerable, not letting others see any personal weaknesses. They actually count on their anger to give them a sense of strength and power. They fixate on judgment of others, themselves, and circumstances. This leads them to become unaware of the reality of a situation or relationship as they focus only on their own opinions and judgments. I think of one gut triad friend who changed jobs more than I can count. Always it was because there was something wrong with the company, her boss, or her job description. Never with herself. An outsider looking in might wonder if she was focusing her attention in the wrong place.

My father was in the gut triad. And just as the Enneagram has helped me personally and in my marriage, it has also helped me as I reflect back on my parents. (I suspect it helps our daughters as they reflect on their parents!) My dad had strong opinions, often negative. His way of "helping" me was to point out what I was doing wrong. Since I live in the heart triad, I was inclined to take most of his opinions personally. Learning about the Enneagram has helped me extend forgiveness to him for his negative control, and extend mercy to myself for feeling hurt. The Enneagram has also helped me appreciate the gifts my father gave to me in his strong abilities and his mastery of life. Even his strong opinions enriched my life.

The disguises of the false self for those in the gut triad are an exaggeration of the gifts of the true self, just as they are for the heart and head triads. Gut people are strong people. But when living in their false self, people in the gut triad use their strength in judgment. They focus on their judgement of other people, ideas, circumstances, and sometimes themselves. Survival for the false self in this triad depends on being in control, on being strong, not weak.

The feeling of drowning in the emotional intensity of the moment leads the false self to escape by trying to control everything with reason and logic. Never mind if this means ignoring the feelings of others or even my own feelings. The false self says that it may be best to ignore reality in order to build its own case and action plan.

Anger attaches itself to the false self in this triad and gives the illusion that it is strong and in power. To the false self for those in this triad, it is better to be angry than to be weak.

As people in the gut triad move toward the true self, they will notice that they approach life with less judgment. Life is not usually an either-or experience. The true self can be both strong and weak. The true self can receive life rather than react to it.

God invites people in this triad to realize that they do not need to be in control all of the time. Life is not about being weak or strong, winning or losing, or being powerful or dependent. It is not either-or but both/and. The apostle Paul had this to say to the early church: "Your attitude should be the same as that of Christ Jesus: Who, being in very nature God, did not consider equality with God something to be grasped, but made himself nothing" (Philippians 2:5-7 NIV 1984). All of us are invited to look to the example of Jesus because all of us, whether we are in the gut triad or not, seek to control life more than we need to.

As people in the gut triad people let go a bit, they find that surrender to God does not wipe them out of existence but gives them true life. God invites them to see themselves as both weak and strong, remembering that on the cross Jesus relinquished power and allowed himself to be weak for the sake of us all. God invites gut triad people to look at life with less judgment, remembering that Jesus healed sinners without judgment. As they let go of the false-self demands for control, judgment, and perfection, people in the gut triad begin to experience peace, serenity, and healthy power in their lives.

LIVING WITH THE ENNEAGRAM

Table 1 puts into perspective how the differences in the three triads influence the way we live and relate to other people. Yes, it is oversimplified. But it gives words to experiences we have every day.

	Heart	Head	Gut
Motivated by	Image (What will others think of me?)	Strategies (How can I solve this?)	Resistance (What is wrong here?)
Focus of attention	Looks out to what others want	Looks within to what I think	Digs in to my own opinion
Life perspective	Life is a task	Life is a problem	Life is a battle
Wants to	Fix the problem	Understand the issue	Control people and circumstances
Instinctive response	"Yes, I'll do that if you want me to."	"I don't know about that. I'll have to think about it."	"No."
Moves	Toward people	Away from people	Against people
Underlying feeling	Shame	Fear	Anger
Seeks	Attention	Security	Autonomy

Table 1. Differences among the triads

Lest the implications of this chart sounds too negative, remember that the Enneagram is not in the business of giving out compliments. After we learn our gifts, we learn a lot about the problems that come with them. If heart triad people want to make connections, it's no surprise that they care a lot about what people think of them. If head triad people are motivated by thinking, it's no surprise that strategies attract them more than action. And if gut triad people want to control, it's not a surprise that they have strong resistance to anything they think is wrong.

Rather than being discouraged by what seems like a negative spin on our gifts, I find that the truth brings freedom. If I do not see the truth in my own life, I become a captive to my blind spots. When I see the truth, I become freer to live with truth or look to God to change me. As a heart triad person, I do not like the energy I put into worrying about what people think of me. I suspect that head triad people do not like their fears about taking action. And gut triad people may wish they were less controlling.

By admitting these characteristics we may not like, we loosen their grip on our lives. We also become freer to accept others in their truth. Philo of Alexandria said, "Be kind, everyone you meet is fighting a great battle."

The truth about ourselves invites us to personal growth. And the truth about others invites us to extend mercy for their weaknesses as well as appreciation for their strengths. Think what this would mean on a church missions committee with only three people, one from each triad. The head triad person might make charts about all the needs on the mission field, compare that to the interests and budget of the church, and suggest that the committee start with lengthy discussions about the various possibilities for giving. The person in the heart triad would probably want to immediately send medical supplies to the needy in Africa, plan a conference (preferably multigenerational) to help people in the church engage in missions, and provide a car for a missionary family coming home on furlough. The one in the gut triad might be irritated that people in the church aren't giving more money, the pastor isn't talking about missions in his sermons more often, and several of the missionaries the church supports aren't doing a better job. If the committee holds a meeting when the false self of each triad shows up, they will spend most of their time arguing about which is the most important perspective to attend to. If, on the other hand, they know that all three committee members have something important to contribute, they can each hold their perspective loosely and offer their gifts for the benefit of the whole group.

LOOKING IN THE MIRROR

Before we go on with the Enneagram, it's time to slow down and look in the mirror. Our journey with the Enneagram will be seriously hindered by going too fast. Even though we need the information provided by the Enneagram, our goal is not information but transformation. And transformation requires stillness and quiet in the presence of the God of grace. Transformation also requires the honesty of authentic self-awareness.

So stop for a few minutes and ask yourself, *So far, what has the Enneagram revealed to me about who I am? Where do I see myself in the triads?* Here are some questions to help you look in the Enneagram mirror.

1. As you look through the characteristics of each triad, notice the things that frequently describe how you live life and relate to others. Make a list of things you identify with, even if they are in different triads. Spend a few minutes musing on these characteristics. Which ones do you like the best? Which ones do you wish were different?

2. Now make a list of the characteristics in the three triads that do not reflect you at all. Stop for a moment and muse on these characteristics. Are there hints of any of these characteristics in your life? Is there a possibility that this list reveals some blind spots? Or does your list help you identify a triad that clearly does not describe you?

3. To help you be honest with yourself about the triads, think about a current, stressful relationship. Spend some time with the three triads to see what insights the Enneagram gives you. What qualities in any of the triads annoy you the most? What qualities in your own triad (if you know it) do you think annoy people close to you? How do any of these annoyances show up in the relationship you are considering? Be quiet for a minute or two and notice if God seems to be inviting you to a different way of seeing yourself or the other person in this relationship.

FOR REFLECTION AND DISCUSSION

1. *The heart triad.* Without naming names, think of someone you know who fits the description of the heart triad. What do you enjoy about that person?

"People in this triad hit roadblocks in life and on their spiritual journey when they begin to feel responsible for the world around them. They feel responsible not only for their own foibles but for the problems of others. This fixation plunges them into anxiety and busyness." If you are a person who feels responsible for other people's problems, what is that like for you?

How do you experience anxious busyness?

"When the false self takes over for people in the heart triad, image becomes all important. What will people think of me? How do I compare to others?" Even if you do not see yourself as a heart triad person, when are you most likely to compare yourself with others?

When are you most likely to hide behind the image you would like to have?

What helps you when image becomes too important?

2. *The head triad.* Without naming names, think of someone you know who seems to fit the description of the head triad. How is this person helpful to you?

"People in the head triad meet roadblocks in their journey when they keep collecting more and more information and allow fear to keep them from acting on their information. They look for safety by continually putting their inner world in order. Even though they may speak of action in the future, it is hard for them to move there." When are you most likely to want to collect more information, guidelines, or experiences?

How does that help you?

How is it unhealthy for you?

"When the roadblocks become overwhelming, the false self rushes in." As they retreat to their minds, head triad people move away from others. Then "the false self feels safe. This attachment to what is going on in the head is a heavy burden to bear." Think of a time when you have been afraid and tried to cope by thinking and strategizing. Was that helpful or unhelpful? How did you know when it became unhelpful?

3. *The gut triad.* Again, without naming names, think of someone you know who seems to live in this triad. How have you benefited from your relationship with this person?

"They see life as a battle to be won and offer their services in leading the charge. Since not everyone else likes to be led into battle, people in the gut triad often meet resistance in their efforts to control other people and circumstances. This leads them to a roadblock of anger." Even if you do not see yourself in the gut triad, you can probably relate to the sense of being resisted by others when you are sure you are right. Think of a time when that happened. How did you feel?

"When the false self takes over for those in this triad, they simply cannot not win. Their very survival depends on being in charge, not being vulnerable, not letting others see any personal weaknesses. They actually count on their anger to give them a sense of strength and power. They fixate on judgment of others, themselves, and circumstances." Avoiding vulnerability, judgmentalism, and anger are all familiar masquerades of the false self for those in the gut triad, but we all experience these temptations to some degree or another. How have you experienced these things in your own life and in relating to others?

4. "The Enneagram, with its triads and spaces, is descriptive, not prescriptive. It makes observations about people in different categories. But it would be a mistake to assume that we can predict how people in each triad or space will respond to life." In what ways do you see the Enneagram as descriptive rather than prescriptive?

5. How have the descriptions of the Enneagram triads been helpful to you so far?

A Personal Meditation
Jesus in the Boat: Mark 4:35-41

On that day, when evening had come, he said to them, "Let us go across to the other side." And leaving the crowd behind, they took him with them in the boat, just as he was. Other boats were with him. A great windstorm arose, and the waves beat into the boat, so that the boat was already being swamped. But he was in the stern, asleep on the cushion; and they woke him up and said to him, "Teacher, do you not care that we are perishing?" He woke up and rebuked the wind, and said to the sea, "Peace! Be still!" Then the wind ceased, and there was a dead calm. He said to them, "Why are you afraid? Have you still no faith?" And they were filled with great awe and said to one another, "Who then is this, that even the wind and the sea obey him?" (NRSV)

To help you picture this passage, you might want to google "Rembrandt Jesus Stills the Storm" to pull up a reproduction of this beautiful painting.

1. If you had been in the boat with Jesus, what do you think you would have been doing during the storm? How might your feelings and actions reflect one of the triads of the Enneagram?

2. How do you respond to Jesus being asleep in the boat?

3. Take a few minutes to muse on Jesus' words "Why are you afraid? Have you still no faith?" For some (especially those in the heart triad) these words might sound harsh. Say them to yourself in the manner and tone of voice that would be most effective for you.

4. What is going on in your life that seems like a threatening storm? How are you responding to the storm? How do you feel about the likelihood that God is "in your boat" right now?

4

The Heart Triad

The Helper, the Achiever, the Individualist

⁓

As the journey continues, we will move deeper into the insights of the Enneagram by looking at the spaces in each triad. These are thumbnail sketches, not intended to completely describe any one person. Different authors have different sketches. You can check out other descriptions of the spaces in the books I have listed in appendix two. But the following descriptions will get us started.

The Enneagram gives words to help us identify our true self as well as our false self. It also gives hints about the movement back and forth between the two, and it suggests the grace God gives to help us participate in that movement. We will start with the heart triad, which means starting with Two. (This is probably annoying to those in the One space, who might prefer to go in proper chronological order, but it is typical of many approaches to the Enneagram.) Remember this is descriptive, not prescriptive. The Enneagram describes how people in each space might look. It is not prescriptive in that the Enneagram does not presume to predict behavior. Even though we necessarily talk about behaviors, the deepest value of the Enneagram is that it just suggests the false-self motivation behind our behaviors.

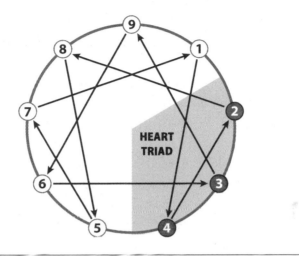

Figure 3. The heart triad

With each triad, you will probably notice that the spaces sound similar but the people in each space express these similarities in different ways. For example, all people in the heart triad care deeply about relationships, but each number lives out their focus on relationships in a unique way. Each space is a nuanced version of the other two spaces in the triad. These nuances are one of the ways the Enneagram is helpful to us. It gives words to the ways we are similar while identifying ways we are different.

THE HELPER· TWO

The Two space expresses the characteristics of the heart triad in living color. They seek out relationships, especially those that give them the opportunity to help others. At their best, people in this space are generous and unselfish. They provide a healing presence in our lives, reflecting that God is loving. Twos are amazing in their desire and ability to help others. They love to connect in self-giving ways. My daughter, who is a Two, was a "helper" in the church nursery when she was only two years old herself. (Today she is on the church staff—in charge of the nursery.) Twos are often in helping professions, but even if not, they will find ways to help others in daily life.

Perhaps because they value connection so much, Twos are very vulnerable to rejection. If they feel you are disappointed in them, or even worse, if they sense that you do not want their help, Twos will scramble to correct the rejection. When this happens, they begin to hit roadblocks in expressing the love of their true self. They may begin to do more talking about what they can and will do for others than actually giving help. They may become overly solicitous and begin to flatter those they want to help or impress. They may even notice, in an honest moment, that they need to be needed in order to feel important.

Taking that a step further, they may believe that God needs them to help out by loving and caring for others. This can lead them to think that God will love them more if they help out. All of this is only a step away from believing that it is not okay for them to have needs themselves. How can I help others if I need to take care of myself? The choice for a Two is, "Am I going to love because I am created to love, or do I believe I have to love in order to be okay?" In other words, for whose sake am I doing this?

Under stress, Twos begin to rescue instead of help, and the false self comes forward. If their efforts are rejected at this point, Twos can become the victims of those they want to help. They may say to themselves, *He just doesn't appreciate me! I'm trying, but I can never seem to do enough! How can she do this to me after all I have done for her!* (The false self likes lots of exclamation points!)

When the false self takes over, Twos become overbearing and manipulative. They can hover, meddle, and control in the name of love. They may become overly intimate and intrusive. They may expect a return for what they give or act like martyrs. They increase their helping activity but feel unappreciated. At this point, they risk losing touch with their natural gentleness and become tough and hard. Twos often feel anger toward those they want to love. They are bewildered by this anger, not realizing that it probably stems from their anger at their own inability to fix or rescue the very people they want to help. But to a Two, anger seems to contradict love, so they cannot admit it. Only when they own up to their anger can they move into a place of being able to love freely.

Pride is the word the Enneagram uses to describe the compulsion (or passion or sin) of the Two false self. They may be proud of the fact that they know what you need, but you do not know what they need. They may be so proud of their perceived ability to solve your problem that they cannot see that you want to solve your problem yourself. Or they may just be proud of all the things they are doing that are working. *How could the world get along without me?* Of course, they dare not admit or show their pride because that would not be loving.

Twos, who are so loving, have a hard time recognizing when their efforts to love do not translate to others as selfless love. Years ago, before I knew the Enneagram, I worked with a woman who must have been a Two. Whenever we had a social event, she was in someone's kitchen. That worked well until it was *my* kitchen. I did not want her fussing around, cleaning up, and putting things in places where I couldn't find them. This same person had a reputation among the Christian students at our local university for picking them up at the bus stop and giving them a ride to school. On a bitterly cold day, this could be welcome help. But once in the car, my friend would grill the student she held captive. "What did you learn from God's Word today? Did you have your quiet time? How are you doing spiritually?" Even though my friend probably thought she was asking these questions because she really loved the students she was helping, the word on the grapevine was that they might have preferred to wait in the cold at the bus stop.

A very dear, very self-aware Two friend told me, "My biggest challenge is not continually initiating contact with people or responding to people who say to me, 'Let's get together sometime.' It's hard for me not to try to live up to others' expectations."

Along the journey of transformation, Twos learn *humility*, the word the Enneagram uses to identify the grace God offers to Twos. They begin to acknowledge that they too are needy and that their own needs may be as important as the needs of others. They embrace their gifts and their limitations. In humility they learn to say, "Maybe I can let someone else do this." "Maybe this person is showing me love in their own way." "Maybe I could do something good for myself too."

One very honest Two told me, "My toughest challenge is being open and vulnerable with others. I would much rather listen to you and take on your burden than put my own feelings into words." In humility, Twos can see that the Spirit of God is loving others through them, but they remember the apostle Paul's words: "We have this treasure in earthen vessels, to show that the transcendent power belongs to God and not to us" (2 Corinthians 4:7 RSV).

I asked another Two friend what she would like people to know about what it's like to be a Two. She said, "I'd like others to know that we love to love and care for people, but we also love to be loved and cared for. When we are able to receive your love and care without qualification, we are often at our best."

Twos are invited, by God's grace, to hold loosely the results of their efforts to love. They are invited to let go of forcing their love on others. And they are invited to love without looking for affirmation, especially when others do not appreciate them as they wish they would. Twos are invited to believe that others can take care of them, just as they desire to care for others. God invites Twos to "approach God's throne of grace with confidence, so that we may receive mercy and find grace to help us in our time of need" (Hebrews 4:16)—mercy for their pride and grace to love themselves and others.

THE ACHIEVER: THREE

People in the Three space are usually very successful. They are good motivators and natural leaders. They are confident, industrious, and ambitious to be the best they can be. They want to be in fashion, trendy, up to date, and popular. They have a healthy drive to get things done and to keep going when the going gets tough. They live to accomplish things and to help others accomplish things. Created in the image of God, they remind us that God, too, accomplishes much and is effective in helping humankind.

Threes motivate themselves and motivate others. I was asked to write an article for a magazine by a friend who is a Three. I said thanks but no thanks. I was too busy at the time. Weeks later as I sat at my computer writing the article, I wondered how I got there. My friend didn't pressure me. But somehow his Three ability to motivate worked. I wrote the article. And I am glad I did.

The question heart triad people are always asking, consciously or unconsciously, is *What do others think of me?* Twos want others to see them as helpful, loving people. Threes want others to see them as successful people. One Three friend told me that her drive for success shows up in some areas of life but not in others. She said she is okay with failure in sports, but she is definitely not okay with failure in a work project. And if she feels she has failed in a relationship, well, "that really hurts."

Growing up, Threes were rewarded for what they did more than for who they were. When Threes ask, "What do you think of me?" (openly or subtly), they probably mean, "Do you think I am doing a good job?" And, in fact, Threes usually are doing a good job! The problem is that they may overly identify with their performance and begin to promote themselves, inflating the importance of their accomplishments. They are generally not drawn to things that do not have external rewards. They may repress their own feelings out of fear of failure. One friend who is a Three says she often pushes herself beyond her limits and runs the risk of physical, emotional, and spiritual exhaustion. She tells me she is good at multitasking, but she can become compulsive about all these tasks, and she needs to remember to regularly unplug. Sabbath rest, with her computer turned off, is important to her.

Underneath this drivenness of the Three is a personal vanity. Like Twos, Threes believe they need to help God get the job done, but their version sounds like this: "Things aren't happening fast enough. God will view me as successful if I do this and help out." Threes believe "I am, therefore I do." This shifts to "I do, therefore I am."

My mother was a Three, and I experienced the positive and negative sides of that space as her daughter. I was proud of all my mother accomplished. I remember my mother's enthusiasm for saving money in order for the whole family to go to Williamsburg. I was grateful for her finding employment in order to finance my college education. But I also lived with the effect of her compulsive busyness and drivenness. Many days I came home from school to sit alone at the dining room table because my mother was out in the community doing things. I also lived with her attempts to impose on me her standards for getting things done. More damage was done as this fed into my own compulsion to spiral into self-doubt. Neither my mother nor I did any of this on purpose. But I wonder how our relationship would have been different if we had each been more self-aware.

If Threes think others are not responding to their efforts, they hustle and bustle to look like they have everything under control.

They put on the mask they think will most likely convince others to think more highly of them. One Three friend said she "puts on her smiley face" when she thinks she is failing at something. Little by little they deny or let go of their own feelings. External image becomes reality for the Three. Under stress, Threes become desperate to avoid failure. They may give into *deceit*, identified by the Enneagram as the compulsion of Threes. They may put a spin on things that twists the truth in order to ensure success. In their deceit, as they lose touch with reality, Threes may become exploitative and opportunistic. They may lose themselves as they imitate others. When their tendency toward competitiveness overwhelms them, Threes may crash. If they are self-aware, they know it is time to take a day off and get in touch with themselves.

Another Three friend said that during a time of crisis in her life, she realized she had been wearing a mask for years. "Certainly there was pain mixed in as I realized how I had been working so hard to keep up appearances. I was living on the unhealthy side of the Three." As painful as it was to admit this, her self-awareness was life giving. God invited her to freedom.

As Threes move toward transformation, they begin to embrace the truth about themselves, their abilities, their weaknesses, and their emotions. They gradually let go of their fear of inadequacy and the threat of failure. They begin to notice when they are craving attention and trying to impress others. *Truth* is the grace identified by the Enneagram to help Threes grow into freedom. God invites them to let go of the grip others' opinions have on them by being truthful about the gifts they have as well as those they don't have. They learn to say, "Maybe what other people think of me isn't so important after all." They become loyal to themselves and not just to their projects. They work cooperatively, for the common good, not just to be personally successful.

As Threes move to follow the example of Jesus, they learn that he was a man who suffered and experienced pain. "He was despised and . . . held . . . in low esteem" (Isaiah 53:3). This is certainly a description that would not please the false self of a Three. But Jesus, spiritually speaking, is the most "successful" person who has ever lived. His success, if we can put it this way, was in his death and resurrection. Indeed, it is only as the false self dies that Threes (and all of the rest of us) can find life and freedom.

THE INDIVIDUALIST: FOUR

People in the Four space are creative, self-aware, intuitive, and sensitive. They value authenticity and sincerity. They see and seek beauty in everyday life. They see each person as unique and special and want others to see them that way. Fours create beautiful spaces, relationally and physically. Created in the image of God, Fours remind us that God is creative.

The creativity of Fours is boundless. It could be expressed in art. (Surely Van Gogh was a Four.) But it could also be expressed in creating a presentation for the workplace or in interior design or landscaping. I have one Four friend, a professor, who expresses his creativity in the courses he designs for his university classes. My spiritual director friends who are Fours create uniquely safe relational spaces for others to speak freely about their spiritual journeys. Fours like to be original.

Fours also ask the question of the heart triad, What do you think of me? The answer they want is a little different from the answer Twos or Threes are looking for. Fours want to be seen as extraordinary: extra ordinary. They dress a little differently. They do ordinary jobs in different ways. They see themselves as different from other people.

Because Fours are motivated by longing for something more special or more beautiful, they focus on what is missing in their lives and in their relationships. This means that melancholy is a frequent experience for Fours. They are sensitive about being misunderstood, which happens quite a bit because they are always trying to be different from everyone else. They may take things too seriously and too personally. They often struggle with self-doubt. They may even think it's not okay to be too happy.

Fours have a magnetic attraction to what is missing or, some would say, to the negative. Ask a Four how his or her vacation was and you may hear how special it was, different from anyone else's vacation. Or, more likely, you will hear all the things that went wrong. I did this myself. One summer we went on a glorious train ride through the Rockies for a week with our children and grandchildren. The scenery was magnificent. The meals were delicious. The grandchildren had fun. The housing was special. What do I remember? The train was late and then got stuck on the tracks by a broken-down freight train. It was hot in the town where we stayed. I didn't get enough sleep. I was worn out by the time we got home. Clearly I would make a terrible travel agent!

When the false self takes over, Fours may withdraw and become self-absorbed. They feel that no one understands them. God is hidden or even absent. This may be because they are more comfortable longing for God than experiencing God. Sometimes my husband says I seem to love him more when he is traveling than when he is home. I wish I didn't do this, but often I seem to enjoy longing for him more than I enjoy his actual presence. I do the same thing with God.

When Fours are living out of the false self, they see the dark side of life. Being willing to explore darkness is a gift the Fours give to others. But it is a bittersweet gift. Darkness is part of the truth of our humanity. But when the false self takes over, a Four sees only darkness. It's a scary thing for Fours to focus on the goodness that is also part of our humanity. What if I stop to look at goodness and something bad comes up behind me before I see it? Using their rich imaginations, Fours can revisit negative experiences endlessly or anticipate negative experiences with such emotion that they undermine their ability to face whatever might be ahead. Mark Twain might remind them, "I am an old man and have known a great many troubles, but most of them never happened."

My own sense is that Fours may feel more secure with the negative. It may give them the illusion of control. They look back and say, "I *knew* that would happen!" Or they look ahead and say, "If I fear the worst, it won't be so bad." But when the dreams and expectations of people in this space fail, they feel inadequate and defective. They may become angry at themselves, and then depressed, feeling alienated from others. This shame can take the form of self-hatred and self-contempt.

The Enneagram identifies the compulsion of the Four as *jealousy* or *envy*. Jealousy is wishing you had what someone else has. Envy is not wanting someone else to have what you want. A subtle distinction, but an honest self-aware Four will recognize both feelings. Riso and Hudson say that "envy causes Fours to see everyone as stable and normal while feeling that they are flawed or, at best, unfinished." The bottom line is that Fours believe they are fundamentally missing what everyone else has.

Equanimity is the gift God offers the Four to move out of this melancholy. Equanimity is a composure under stress. Or, as Russ Hudson said at a conference on the Enneagram, "Equanimity is a spaciousness of the heart that lets me feel whatever needs to be felt without rejecting the feeling or adhering to it, not pushing it away or getting stuck in it." A Four, then, is invited to notice feelings of inadequacy, being misunderstood, or being jealous of all that others have, and then stop long enough to let go of those feelings. This is so much easier said than done, but it is a starting point.

I sometimes say to myself, *Okay, Self, you go act like a Four. I have to get on with life!*

At one workshop I attended, a wise Four gave us two quotes that I needed to write down. The first is an idiom I had never heard before: "There is less to this than meets the eye." The second is a quote from *The Hiding Place* by Robert Shaw: "Situation hopeless, but not serious." Both of these quotes should be hanging on the wall of my mind. (I realize that those who are not Fours may think these quotes are misquotes, but if in doubt, ask a Four!)

Jesus said, "If you're content to be simply yourself, you will become more than yourself" (Luke 18:14 *The Message*). This is an invitation for everyone in the heart triad, but I believe it is a special invitation to Fours. As Fours move toward transformation, they learn that they are already original, that they don't need to become more special, more authentic, more unique. They learn to be content with what they have and who they are. They begin to experience a calmness and equilibrium that grows from equanimity. They learn, to their surprise, that happiness can, at least occasionally, be theirs.

FOR REFLECTION AND DISCUSSION

1. *The Helper: Two.* Summarize the perspective of those in the Two space. What motivates them the most?

   What are the particular temptations of the false self for those in this space?

   Define the grace offered to those in this space. What might that grace looked like as it is lived out in daily life?

   How have you experienced the characteristics of this space in your own life or in the lives of those you know and love?

2. *The Achiever: Three.* Summarize the perspective of those in the Three space. What motivates them the most?

What are the particular temptations of the false self for those in this space?

Define the grace offered to those in this space. What might that grace looked like as it is lived out in daily life?

How have you experienced the characteristics of this space in your own life or in the lives of those you know and love?

3. *The Individualist: Four.* Summarize the perspective of those in the Four space. What motivates them the most?

What are the particular temptations of the false self for those in this space?

Define the grace offered to those in this space. What might that grace looked like as it is lived out in daily life?

How have you experienced the characteristics of this space in your own life or in the lives of those you know and love?

A Personal Meditation
Jesus Serving Dinner: Luke 12:35-37

This parable is often seen as a future event, but as with all of Jesus' stories, there is hidden truth that can enrich our lives right now. Take a few minutes to consider this amazing event.

> *Be dressed ready for service and keep your lamps burning, like servants waiting for their master to return from a wedding banquet, so that when he comes and knocks they can immediately open the door for him. It will be good for those servants whose master finds them watching when he comes. Truly I tell you, he will dress himself to serve, will have them recline at the table and will come and wait on them.*

1. What do you think you would have been doing if you had been one of these servants waiting for the arrival of the Master? How does the perspective of your Enneagram space influence your life as a servant of Christ?

2. What would you have thought and felt when the Master walked in and had you recline at the table so he could wait on you? Spend some time picturing that scene.

3. Think of the table before you as a metaphor for the things Jesus might want to give you today. What is Jesus offering you? (Would you like a bowl of love? Or try this delicious peace. Or here, try this—I made it especially for you.)

4. Spend some time in conversation with God about this event. How do you feel about Jesus serving you? How would you like God to be at work in you to help you receive this gift? What do you want to say to God about this parable?

Now be quiet, and just listen to the whispers of God in your heart and mind.

5

The Head Triad

The Observer, the Loyalist, the Enthusiast

P eople in the head triad are surprised to find out that not everyone approaches life as they do. "Why," they say, "would anyone *not* base their life, their decisions, and their relationships on what they *think*? Surely what we think about life is most

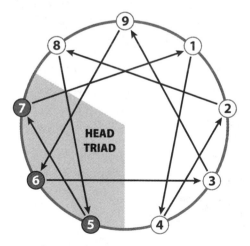

Figure 4. The head triad

important." Those of us in other triads could probably explain to them that what goes on in their heads does not make the world go round. But our explanations would not be good enough for them. And, as we shall see, people in each space of the head triad think differently about the things they value.

THE OBSERVER: FIVE

Created in the image of God, Fives remind us that God is wise and that wisdom is a gift God gives to creation. Fives have amazing perceptiveness and insight. They are often visionaries in their comprehension of the world. They tend to be serious and value privacy, but at their best they have wisdom that comes from experiential engagement with the world. (When they disengage, their "wisdom" becomes theoretical.) Fives want to get at the essence of things. When my husband and I read the same book, he pays attention to the concepts and principles. I pay attention to the personal examples.

I found out how helpful Bob's wisdom is early in our marriage. We were in campus ministry and discovered that when young people come to college, they not only go to class but may also fall in love and get engaged. Many of these newly engaged couples landed on our doorstep to ask for advice. Never mind that we had been married barely a year ourselves. We would meet with couples for premarital counseling in our living room. Immediately I engaged them in conversation, pouring my heart out trying to help them understand the strengths and weaknesses of their relationship. Bob sat in the chair opposite me and listened in on the conversation we were having. Just when I thought I was in this all alone, Bob would speak up. "Well," he would say, "the way I see it is . . ." Then he would observe what he heard in the conversation. When the couple stood up to leave, almost every time one of them would say, "Thank you so much. It was all helpful, but what Bob said at the end was the most helpful." Even though I ate humble pie, I knew, in my better moments, that Bob couldn't have gotten to his summary without my having engaged the couple in their life story. Bob was there, but waiting until the stories were over and he felt that he had a handle on the "issues." Then he would speak up.

For people in the Five space, engagement takes an intentional effort. If that doesn't happen, Fives can detach from people and retreat into their thoughts. They move away and watch from a safe hiding place in their minds. The body may be present, but the mind is someplace else. When our teenage daughters would ramble on at the dinner table about things that didn't seem very important to Bob, I could often see him slipping away. A swift kick under the table sometimes helped.

Fives, then, may choose to retreat into the sanctuary of their thinking. They may begin to hoard knowledge in an effort to fill an inner sense of emptiness. They become preoccupied with their own interpretations of reality, and it may be hard for them to engage in life. They often believe that they cannot risk taking action until they have carefully thought about what they might do. In the meantime, others have moved on, much to the Five's dismay.

One of the bewildering effects of Fives' hoarding of knowledge is that they sometimes seem stingy, having an air of superiority, even though they see themselves as very loving people. They may believe, "I need to learn everything I can about God and about life by observing, analyzing, and theorizing. Then God, and everyone else, will see me as wise and worthwhile."

That, of course, is the false self putting a foot in the door. When the false self takes over, Fives begin to take an antagonistic and critical stance toward anything that interferes with their inner world and personal vision. A fear of powerlessness may lead them to focus on issues they think they can master in their minds. They may become reclusive and isolated. God appears to them more like an idea than a person. Feeling inadequate, they come to believe that knowledge, time alone, and personal insights will make up for their deficiencies. Hoarding their knowledge, they give in to *avarice* or *greed*, the compulsion the Enneagram identifies in the Five space. Fives tell me that feeling greedy about their knowledge spills over into greed in other areas of life, including time, money, and energy. At this point, Fives want to take in wisdom (and life), but they don't want to give anything out.

The Enneagram identifies the gift given to Fives to help them out of this dilemma as *detachment*. This may seem odd to the Five who has just discovered that it is a problem when he or she detaches from other people. But the kind of detachment the Enneagram is suggesting is a detachment from the ideas Fives are hoarding. Detachment in this sense is holding their wisdom and perceptions loosely. It is a letting go of the fear that others will take advantage of them. It is a letting go of escaping into the mind and believing that they need to know everything before taking action. It is detachment from what they think they need instead of a grasping for life. This is the kind of detachment the Enneagram is inviting Fives to experience.

When Fives detach in healthy ways, they are freer to own their own emotional needs, something that is difficult for Fives to do. At one workshop I attended, the presenter, a Five himself, suggested that people in this space need to keep it simple when looking at their feelings. Am I glad, sad, mad, or scared? (This is quite different from the list of one hundred emotions I like to look at.) Healthy Fives can risk being more transparent about their feelings. They learn to engage with others even if they don't know everything about the situation. They let go of preconceived notions about other people. They learn to be open to what is in front of them and to trust their own spontaneous responses.

Sometimes Fives put other people off with their far-reaching wisdom and strong opinions. But Fives tell me that it is hurtful when others do not want to hear their thinking and their perceptions. This is what they have to offer. They feel that they have something worthwhile to bring to the table, but no one wants to listen to them. This can cause them to withdraw even more or to push their thoughts and opinions onto their colleagues. Neither option works. As with all the Enneagram spaces, Fives are invited to offer what they have to give and then notice if what they are offering is life giving to those in other spaces. As they engage with others, they are freer to offer their wisdom effectively and lovingly.

Fives, by God's grace, are invited to trust the truth in James's letter to the early church: "If any of you lacks wisdom, you should ask God, who gives generously to all without finding fault, and it will be given to you" (James 1:5). According to James, not only does God give wisdom, but God does not find fault with us, even when we do not know and understand everything. This, indeed, is grace.

THE LOYALIST: SIX

The name says it all. Sixes are loyal people. At their best, they are courageous and positive. They trust both themselves and others. They are responsible and friendly. They remind us that God is faithful and that faithfulness is one of the fruits of God's Holy Spirit.

My mother-in-law was certainly a Six. Looking back, I wonder what she thought when Bob chose a wife who was so different from his parents. I brought new perspectives and new possibilities into the family. Now I know how difficult that must have been. But Bob's mother loved me. She appreciated me. She was loyal to me. Her loyalty and love invited me into a more loving relationship with God.

When Sixes are living out of the true self, out of a healthy place, they believe that the world is out to do them good. They believe that God's will is unfolding within them. In this faith, their courage grows. When they are living out of the false-self perspective, Sixes feel they can no longer trust the world or themselves. They believe that they must get God on their side or they will get hurt. Some Sixes, in moments of healthy self-awareness, would say they have so lost touch with their own inner authority that they don't even have a "side." They look to someone else to find out what to do, what to think, what to decide. When this happens, fear replaces courage. Richard Rohr says that all people deal with fear, but Sixes "make an art form of it."

One Six friend described the fear she feels when presented with a new idea. If this idea is different from what she already believes, she is afraid she will be totally derailed. She feels threatened that a new, different idea will invalidate all the other things she believes. She discussed this fear with her spiritual director. He made the passing comment, "Well, you don't have to believe the new idea." It was not as though she had never heard that obvious truth before. But this time, the truth broke through the negative side of her Enneagram stance, which looks compulsively to others for authority. She could become her own authority. She could choose to agree or disagree with the new idea. By God's grace, she could trust her own judgment. This possibility was life changing for my friend.

The Enneagram identifies *fear* as the compulsion of the Six. Their loyalty is rooted in the fear of being without the support they believe they need. Sixes also live with a low-level cowardice about life. They believe they need to be prepared for every possible danger. The worst-case scenario is just around the corner. They do not believe that they have the inner strength or resources to deal with life, so Sixes look outside themselves to find security—to rules, traditions, organizations, even theology. Without realizing it, they believe that God always agrees with those in authority and that God wants to keep the status quo. Sixes believe it is their job to help God do that.

As they come to rely too much on authority outside themselves, Sixes have trouble making their own decisions. I met with a self-professed Six for spiritual direction. She was struggling with a life-changing decision. For months she talked about all the pros and cons, dissecting and analyzing all the possible outcomes, as head triad people are prone to do. Then one day I asked her, "What are you afraid of about this decision?" The conversation changed from worst-case scenarios to her fears. It turned out to be a helpful change. Noticing what she was afraid of allowed her to talk about the things that were keeping her from deciding. She was able to move on and make a good choice.

One of the interesting, and confusing, things about people in this space is that most Sixes are overly submissive to authority. But some express their focus on authority by being rebellious, doing just the opposite of what the authority might say. Two different Sixes could be driving down the highway, one driving 59 miles an hour in a 60-mile-per-hour speed limit and the other going 80 miles per hour just because the authority says the limit is 60 miles per hour. For both of them, it is their focus on authority that is motivating their behavior.

Submissive Sixes are called phobic Sixes, and rebellious Sixes are called counter-phobic Sixes. Both phobic and counter-phobic Sixes live with chronic fear but in different ways. Usually phobic Sixes have some sense that fear is motivating them. Counter-phobic Sixes are less aware of their fear. As they aggressively do the opposite of what the authority says, they are end-running the "rules" rather than admitting their underlying fear of being abandoned by those in authority. It is a mysterious phenomenon for those of us who are not in this space. Phobic Sixes are statistically more common, but counter-phobic Sixes tell me they need to be heard too.

I asked a Six friend how the Enneagram had helped him. He said, "Often my tendency to fear is almost unconscious, but the Enneagram helps me be more aware of it. The Enneagram also helps me be aware of when courage overcomes fear and I can provide leadership to people and groups and help in managing projects." Another friend said she has learned from the Enneagram that fear is the root of her desire to control. She tries to control her own life and others in order to avoid disapproval and to feel secure. This self-awareness has helped her come to God for what she needs instead of expecting it from her family and friends.

Sixes are often afraid to believe that you love them. Perhaps they are so busy looking out for danger that they can't stop long enough to receive love. Or perhaps they believe that love, like authority, comes with strings attached and expectations of obedience.

I asked my Six friends what they would like others to know about what it is like to be a Six. One friend said, "Please don't dismiss/berate my fears and my struggle to trust God with certain things, especially when those things are easy for you to trust God for." This means that when we engage with Sixes, it is probably not helpful to remind them that Jesus said "Fear not!" even though that is true. We can love Sixes by listening to their fears, accepting them in their struggles, and allowing God's love, often through our listening, to bring healing.

As Sixes move toward transformation, they receive the grace of *courage*. They learn to trust themselves and others. They are not afraid to believe they are loved. They learn to be as attentive to themselves as they are to outside influences. They learn that their fears may not be grounded in reality. Sixes in transformation learn to go with the flow, trust the process, and follow the spirit of the law rather than the letter of the law. In transformative moments, they discover the courage to trust themselves and find out that they can truly have faith in God's work within them as well as in other people. At moments like this they can say to themselves, with the psalmist, "Be strong, and let your heart take courage, all you who wait for the LORD!" (Psalm 31:24 RSV).

THE ENTHUSIAST: SEVEN

People in the Seven space are fun to be around. They enjoy life. They are optimistic and look for the silver lining in all things. At their best they remind us that God is joyful. Indeed, joy is one of the gifts of the Holy Spirit.

The wife of a Seven told me about her husband the day after a significant blizzard in her area. A professional man and a grandfather, he was nowhere to be found. Thinking he might have gone out to clear the driveway, she looked out the front window. There he was, by himself, lying down in the front yard making snow angels. As any self-respecting Seven would say, you don't need grandchildren to have fun.

Another Seven told me of a time when she went out to dinner. She ordered every dessert on the menu. She assured me that she didn't eat them all herself. She just wanted to see what they were and have a taste of them. Then she shared them with her friends. It was a great, sweet experience.

Fun, for most Sevens, takes precedence over everything. My friend Carol works with a Seven. She loves the fun part, but she also bumps into the negative side of her Seven colleague. (As is often the case, we see the compulsions in someone else more clearly than we see our own.) "For instance," Carol said, "he told me he was about to resign because the company was not allowing him to take days off when he wanted to, even though he limited himself to the number of days off allowed by our policy. We were able to keep him on staff only by allowing him to take off when he chose to." My friend added that her colleague "fills his life to the very edges, saying yes to every good thing. In all the years I've known him, I've only known him to say no one time."

I was surprised at first to see the name given to the Seven space by Don Riso in *Enneagram Transformations*. He identifies this space as "The Generalist: The Hyperactive, Uninhibited Type." That doesn't sound very joyful or nice to me, but then I remembered that the Enneagram is not in the business of handing out compliments. Riso goes on to say that Sevens "try to escape from their fear of being deprived by immersing themselves in constant activity." They fear, he says, "that if they run out of stimulation—of things to have and do—something terrible will happen." Again, this is illustrative of Enneagram teaching. The gifts of our true self are threatened by the fears of our false self, and all human beings risk becoming compulsive about those fears. Sevens are joyful people, but if they listen to their false self, they assume they need to be compulsively stimulated in order to maintain that joy.

For Sevens it is more effective to be optimistic than pessimistic. This is true for many situations, but when Sevens overstate the positive, they can become compulsively optimistic and ignore the possible reality in the negative. Sevens are also easily bored. They are good at starting things up, but when things get going, they may disengage and head out. Sevens avoid life by dreaming and planning. They are more comfortable dreaming in their heads than looking at something in depth.

When the false self takes over, Sevens deny pain and sadness. They simply don't trust darkness. They will not tolerate pessimism. In their fear of the dark, Sevens escape into *gluttony*, the compulsion the Enneagram identifies for them. Gluttony is an insatiable desire for more. In their desperation to avoid pain, Sevens take in as many distractions as they can by collecting things or experiences. They don't let themselves be satisfied by anything because that might mean slowing down the compulsive quest for more and more possible entertainments.

I asked a Seven friend what he liked about being a Seven. He was quick to say that he liked being able to see the silver lining in most situations. That, he said, has helped him make and keep friends, in spite of being introverted. (Most, but not all, Sevens are extroverts. It's great to see my friend express his Seven gifts in his own introverted way.) Then I asked him what frustrated him about being in the Seven space. He said that it's frustrating to be so focused on future plans that he's not always present to the people around him. He also notices that he is quick to want new things before thinking through whether or not it is something he really needs. In these observations, my friend is using his knowledge of the Enneagram to become more self-aware, noticing the good as well as the not so good in himself. His ability to embrace the good and the bad is a challenging and life-giving experience.

On the journey to transformation Sevens learn the grace of *sobriety*. Sobriety means taking only what we need. But it also means an attitude of seriousness or dignity. Both of these perspectives hold an invitation to the Seven. They are invited to let go of the feeling that they never have enough, that they always need more. They are invited to use and enjoy what they already have. They are also invited to a sobriety or seriousness about life that allows them to embrace pain and disappointment. Life is not always fun. It is not always exciting. Sometimes it is boring. Sevens are invited to stay in the present, to hold their dreams loosely so that they will not over-plan and then not finish what they've planned. They are invited to slow down so they have the time and space to notice what really satisfies them and what merely tempts them. I asked a very articulate Seven friend how the Enneagram has helped her. She said, "It has given me the ability to live as if there is enough of everything. I can settle back into a chair in my mind instead of sitting at the edge of the chair as if I would miss what matters."

Riso says that Sevens need to "learn to stay with each experience long enough to assimilate it." Then, he says, they "finally realize that no experience or thing in the external world can ultimately keep them satisfied or free from anxiety." And this, Riso says, will lead them to find within themselves "a stillness and serenity which is a dependable source of undiminished joy."

For the Seven, then, the gift of joy they give to the world comes when they let go of the compulsive ways they try to make themselves happy. They have already been given joy, and they don't need more joy in order to give it away to others. Eugene Peterson calls joy an "exuberance about life" (Galatians 5:22 *The Message*). This exuberance is what my Seven friends offer to me. I am thankful for them.

FOR REFLECTION AND DISCUSSION

1. *The Observer: Five.* Summarize the perspective of those in the Five space. What motivates them the most?

   What are the particular temptations of the false self for those in this space?

   Define the grace offered to those in this space. What might that grace looked like as it is lived out in daily life?

   How have you experienced the characteristics of this space in your own life or in the lives of those you know and love?

2. *The Loyalist: Six.* Summarize the perspective of those in the Six space. What motivates them the most?

   What are the particular temptations of the false self for those in this space?

Define the grace offered to those in this space. What might that grace looked like as it is lived out in daily life?

How have you experienced the characteristics of this space in your own life or in the lives of those you know and love?

3. *The Enthusiast: Seven.* Summarize the perspective of those in the Seven space. What motivates them the most?

What are the particular temptations of the false self for those in this space?

Define the grace offered to those in this space. What might that grace looked like as it is lived out in daily life?

How have you experienced the characteristics of this space in your own life or in the lives of those you know and love?

A Personal Meditation
Feeding the Five Thousand: Mark 6:38-44

And he said to them, "How many loaves have you? Go and see." When they had found out, they said, "Five, and two fish." Then he ordered them to get all the people to sit down in groups on the green grass. So they sat down in groups of hundreds and of fifties. Taking the five loaves and the two fish, he looked up to heaven, and blessed and broke the loaves, and gave them to his disciples to set before the people; and he divided the two fish among them all. And all ate and were filled; and they took up twelve baskets full of broken pieces and of the fish. Those who had eaten the loaves numbered five thousand men. (NRSV)

---

1. We live in a society that fears scarcity. What are you most afraid of running out of—money, time, energy, power, or something else?

2. Clarence Thomson says that we "presuppose a world in which there isn't enough of whatever it is that I want. My Enneagram style," he says, "is a style in which I have to work terribly hard to get what I am utterly devoted to." How do your own fears of scarcity reflect the stance of your Enneagram triad or space?

3. Who do you identify with the most in this passage—the disciples, the people in the crowd, or Jesus? What feelings would you have had if you had been part of this event?

4. When in the past have you actually ended up with more than enough of whatever you most fear running out of? Take some time to ponder the possibility that you already have enough of everything you need today. In what areas of your life might this be true?

5. Sit quietly for a few minutes picturing yourself in this event. Picture Jesus noticing you and walking up to you. What might Jesus say to you?

The Gut Triad

The Challenger, the Peacemaker, the Perfectionist

～✦

N ow we move to the gut triad, an interesting triad indeed. Just as people in the head triad are surprised that other people may not look at life primarily through their minds, people in the gut triad are surprised that other people may not see the love

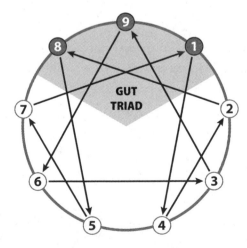

Figure 5. The gut triad

behind their strength and strong opinions. Why wouldn't someone want to know the right thing to do? We will see how each space in the gut triad expresses their strength and confidence in a different way.

THE CHALLENGER: EIGHT

Created in the image of God, Eights reflect the power of their Creator. At their best they use their power to help the disenfranchised. Eights are assertive, confident, and independent. They stand up for what they want and need, for themselves and for those they companion. They reflect the truth that God is not only powerful, God is just.

Eights provide leadership in many settings: in the office, at home, in the community, and at church. They come to conclusions about what is needed and respond strongly and quickly. Sometimes they offer their leadership skills in the ordinary events of life. Sometimes they jump in when there is an emergency. Often they use their leadership to help those in need.

John told me about a Eight in his church. His friend was a highly successful businessman, a consultant for an international company. He was opinionated and had the "push against" quality of the Eight, but he also exhibited real care for the underdog. In fact, John told me that this man was a key player in starting their church, mainly because he saw the effect of abuse in a former church. John's friend used his leadership gifts to start the new church as a place that would redeem and protect those abused by a former church leader. Not everyone would be able to take on care for others of this magnitude, but healthy Eights have much to offer all of us.

Another friend, a very self-aware Eight, remembers that as a child she felt protective of her younger sister, who had Down Syndrome. "When I was about nine, I remember beating up a kid who was older and bigger than me when he started to call her names." She assures me that as an adult she no longer resorts to violence, but she still appreciates the energy of her Eight space, which gives her the strength to defend the weak. People in the Eight space often say they like to use their gifts to help those who are not able to help themselves.

Eights see things in black and white. They assess situations quickly and move in with the solution. This is great when it is needed. But it doesn't work so well when Eights become compulsive. The temptation for the Eight is to believe "It's my way or the highway." People who work with those in this space may become frustrated at their unwillingness to see any other solutions than the one they believe in.

When Eights hit roadblocks in life, they are likely to ignore their own tender feelings and to deny their own vulnerability. Being weak is just not an option for a frustrated Eight. They do not want to be submissive to someone else. They can be blunt and confrontational, needing to win and to dominate. At this point they probably don't listen well. Eights think that they are strong, fair, honest, and tough. They believe that other people need them. Problems arise when others disagree with that assessment.

If you try to engage in a power play with an unhealthy Eight, you are in trouble. They will take justice into their own hands. One Eight said that she is "a fixer, implementation specialist, a doer." She said, "I love challenges and finding solutions to problems, creating efficiencies." But she is noticing that this doesn't always work, especially with her children. "Some things do not need to be fixed, and efficiencies aren't the end game, so bracketing those tendencies is necessary." She is learning to sit with unanswered questions. Although this is a challenge for an Eight, she finds that it brings her peace, remembering that "I don't have to do anything. God is holding it."

When Eights forget this and live out of the false self, they give in to their lust for more and more power. *Lust*, according to the Enneagram, is the passion of the Eight. They can recklessly over-extend themselves and become hardhearted, even immoral and violent. They don't trust anyone and become territorial. They don't pick fights, but they will fight if you get in their territory.

At their best, then, Eights use their power to serve others. At their worst, they become manipulative and overbearing. At their best, they think before they speak or act. In their false self, they may drop out if they don't think they can win. (Think of the powerful person in a business meeting who closes his laptop, sits back, and declares, "If that's what you plan to do, you'll have to do it on your own! I'm out of here.")

Not surprisingly, the gift of grace to the Eight is *innocence*. According to Dr. Jerry Wagner, innocence is a childlike capacity to experience "each moment fresh without expectations and pre-judgments." Seeing life with innocence is the opposite of the compulsive lust of the Eight. Wagner says that lust means "you do everything to excess. You can be possessive, grabby, and demanding." As those in this space move forward on the journey of transformation, they begin to hold their judgments more loosely and receive the life-changing possibilities of each moment.

People who are not in the Eight space may wonder what it's like to approach life with such a powerful perspective. I asked some Eight friends what they would like others to know about being in this space. One told me that "if you want to work well with an Eight, don't come at them. This oppositional energy toward them will only raise their guard and make them ready to fight. Instead come next to them. Assume you are on the same team, and communicate that you need their help in bringing change, saving the world, protecting the weak."

Another person had the self-awareness to know that "while I think I'm relational and sensitive, most people experience me as overpowering, intimidating, and very self-assured. Often I am not aware of my power over/on others." She said she appreciates when someone who loves her and knows her well gives her that feedback. Not everyone can do that for an Eight, but my friend said her husband gives her that gift.

The Bible teaches that the lion and the lamb will one day live together (Isaiah 11:6). Weakness and strength belong with each other (2 Corinthians 12:9-10). As Eights embrace God's grace, they begin to experience this truth. They learn to say, "Maybe I don't need to be in charge. Maybe I can let my guard down a bit. Maybe I can let my heart be touched more deeply." As they move in this direction, they experience the freedom and simplicity of innocence. And they become great leaders.

THE PEACEMAKER: NINE

People in the Nine space are calm people, at ease with life. At their best they are content and even-tempered, and they trust others and themselves. They are a peaceful influence, bringing harmony to individuals and groups. Nines remind us that God is peaceful.

One Nine friend said that she likes bringing "a peaceful energy into settings, having a calming effect on those around me." Another Nine said, "I like being a calm and peaceful presence." Someone else told me, "I like having a slower pace of life, seeing both sides of an issue, and being a good listener." The Nines in my life have all given me these gifts.

Nines might say to us, "Don't push the river; it flows by itself." But, as we find out in our friendships with Nines, they do not like to be pushed themselves. They have developed a protective self that exaggerates peace. When they feel threatened or pushed, they may retreat. They can become indolent, an impressive word that means they "avoid exertion." Some of us make mountains out of molehills. Nines make molehills out of mountains. And when they hit roadblocks, Nines are tempted to shut down. They become paralyzed, unable to move toward decision, especially if that decision might cause conflict. One Nine I know goes away to her cottage when things get too stressful or complicated.

Growing up, Nines may have felt abused in the face of anger, and they do not want to impose anger on anyone else. Anger is there, but they repress it. This explains the confusing placement of the peaceful Nine space right between the Eight and the One spaces, where anger is more obvious. The peaceful stance of the Nine looks like an anomaly in the gut triad. But self-aware Nines tell us the anger is there. Some will even say they feel a rage deep inside their being; it just doesn't show. But keeping it hidden is usually not helpful for those in this space. In fact, self-aware Nines tell me that acknowledging and expressing their anger is life giving for them. One friend said, "I'm not always as calm on the inside as I appear to be on the outside. I've learned that anger is a motivator for me, and if I get angry, it's a good (and rare) thing."

Because Nines work so hard to avoid conflict, they may feel left out. If expressing an opinion means disagreement and potential conflict, a Nine will be silent. When Nines say, "Oh, it doesn't matter," they may mean, "I don't matter." Nines, then, often feel unimportant, not realizing that they have sabotaged themselves.

When Nines give in to the false self and dissociate from all conflict, they give in to the compulsion of *sloth* or laziness. In the not-very-flattering vernacular, they risk becoming couch potatoes. They ignore potential problems and focus on their desire for peace rather than accomplishment. They lose touch with a sense of being loved because they feel they don't matter anyhow. They may say to themselves, *I won't let this get to me* so the pain/sadness/anger doesn't hurt so much.

Some teachers of the Enneagram have noticed a similarity between the Nine and the Two. People in both spaces ignore themselves by giving in to the needs and requests of others. The difference is that Twos want recognition and appreciation for their sacrifice, and Nines are embarrassed by being noticed and acknowledged.

When Nines take the journey of transformation, they begin to move into *action*. As they tap into their own anger, they may find the energy to move off the couch of indecision and inaction. As they begin to allow themselves to be noticed and loved, they begin to love others in constructive ways. And as they begin to trust their own perspective, they generate their inner confidence instead of draining off others' energy.

One Nine said it this way: "For me, moving toward health and freedom has been about finding myself, valuing me, and being present to my thoughts, desires, and feelings." She added, "This has been difficult because . . . it was safer to not desire, not feel, and to think that nothing really matters so I wouldn't feel disappointment." But, she said, "Finding support from others who encourage me to express my desires, opinions, and feelings has brought much healing."

As Nines move toward transformation, they find they are not solely responsible for keeping peace in the world. And they find that peace may be beyond their own perspective. They find that "the peace of God, which transcends all understanding" guards their hearts and their minds in Christ Jesus (Philippians 4:7).

Those of us who know and love Nines will want to encourage them on this journey. I asked a friend what she would like people to know about being a Nine. She said, "Nine space people may seem very different and aloof; however, they just want to be accepted for who they are and to be invited in. We have a lot to contribute. . . . Nines are easily passed by. Notice and see them."

The gift of peace, which Nines bring into our world, is indeed a gift we want to notice.

THE PERFECTIONIST: ONE

People in the One space have very high standards. At their best they are conscientious and ethical. They have strong personal convictions that reflect the value they give to truth and excellence. They remind us that God is good and that goodness is one of the fruits of the Holy Spirit (Galatians 5:22).

For Ones, anything worth doing is worth doing well. They envision the perfectly good thing and are not satisfied with anything less. All of life is met with high moral standards. Unfortunately Ones shift from wanting to do all things well to believing they must do all things well. This leads them to decide that they must be perfect themselves. For Ones, then, even more than for the rest of us, perfectionism drives their lives. When Ones hit roadblocks in life and find they cannot do everything perfectly, they become resentful. They try to improve everything, to make it what it "ought" to be. They criticize themselves and others for missing the mark.

My father was a One, and I grew up with his perfect standards and his "loving" criticism. Many times I chafed under his pronouncements. Now I know that when he was correcting me or telling me how I could improve on what I was doing, he was loving me in the way of a One. I also know that for self-aware Ones this propensity to be critical is the bane of their existence. But the criticisms others feel are nothing compared to the criticisms Ones have of themselves. Ones tell me they are frustrated that they think they are never good enough. They can always think of a way something could have been done better.

In fact, this chronic desire to be better seems to lead Ones to be dissatisfied with being Ones. When I asked a few Ones what they liked about being in the One space, one person answered, "The question caught me by surprise. I usually think of being a One as something I need to work hard to overcome." Another said, "Nothing!" Apparently Ones cannot even be at home in their space. They can always improve.

But my One friends went on to say that they did like being self-disciplined and being able to work to correct injustices. People who work with Ones can attest to the benefits of having people on the team who pay attention to details and keep working to do things well.

The false self appears when Ones come to believe that everything can be improved and nothing is good enough. They begin to experience *anger*, especially toward themselves but also toward others. When the false self takes over, Ones can become rigid, demanding, and critical. One person told me that he is frustrated by his dualistic, either-or approach to life. This leads him to being too judgmental and exclusive. Another One said that her false-self energy is that of a "Pharisee of Pharisees." Like the Pharisees of the New Testament, my friend says she often sees things as right or wrong, black or white. "My arrogance," she said, "can seep into the 'cracks' and I can be oblivious of it until it is running all over me. I become terrified that I will cause someone to feel condescended and dishonored." This, to me, is wonderful and helpful self-awareness.

When Ones try to fight this resentment and anger head-on, they often resort to rationalizing their own actions. Another risk is that they turn their anger onto themselves and become depressed. When they step back from their anger and notice how their judgments reflect an unrealistic perfectionism, they can begin to stop blaming themselves and others.

Some people notice that Ones and Sixes both try to compulsively do things right or correctly. The difference is that Sixes decide what is right based on what an outer authority says. Ones decide what is right based on their own sense of inner authority, which often has an unrealistic standard.

Ones think they need to have the "right" answer first, down to the smallest thing. I heard of a One who even struggled to let her young daughter win a game. In the grown-up world, she struggled to have a solution to whatever concrete issue someone else presented, whether it was about computers, organizational policy, or what product to use to solve the current office problem. Looking in from outside the One space, we can only imagine the burden this would be.

This is why *serenity* is the grace offered to Ones. Serenity allows Ones to receive life rather than react to it. Life is what it is, not what could be better. (A shocking possibility to those in the One space!) As Ones journey toward transformation, they find themselves able to live life with more patience and compassion. They hold life more loosely, even playfully.

Ones gravitate to the words of Jesus often translated, "Be perfect, therefore, as your heavenly Father is perfect" (Matthew 5:48). "Of course!" Ones might say. "That's what I've been telling you all along." But others translate these words with a little more clarity. The Common English Bible says, "Therefore, just as your heavenly Father is complete in showing love to everyone, so also you must be complete." *The Message* says it this way: "Live generously and graciously toward others, the way God lives toward you."

According to my commentaries, the biblical word often translated "perfect" also means "complete." Perfection is static. God is not static, but God is complete. We have a complete revelation of God's goodness to us today. But God's grace reveals itself anew in every life event. Paul said, "Not a day goes by without his unfolding grace" (2 Corinthians 4:16 *The Message*). The way we experience grace today is a little different from the way we experienced it yesterday. As Ones move more deeply into God's love, they discover that, for today, they have all they need to live in grace. They do not need to look for perfection. Grace will be revealed again tomorrow. This allows them to respond to life with serenity.

I asked my One friends what they would like us to know about this journey to grace and serenity. One friend said that as she takes this journey, she'd like others to know that she is sorry she can be so demanding: "If I have high expectations for you, please know that I have even higher expectations of myself. Don't walk away and leave me with all the work. Help me to laugh at myself and trust that it will be okay." Another friend said that her spiritual director helps her see goodness in herself that she cannot see on her own: "Without someone holding that mirror up for me to see, I would be lost to accepting what is and left swirling around in a judgment whirlwind . . . in a never-ending effort to fix myself and others."

As Ones give the gift of their high standards for goodness in the world, we can return their gift with grace as they, like all of us, journey deeper into the generosity and love of God.

FOR REFLECTION AND DISCUSSION

1. *The Challenger: Eight.* Summarize the perspective of those in the Eight space. What motivates them the most?

   What are the particular temptations of the false self for those in this space?

   Define the grace offered to those in this space. What might that grace look like as it is lived out in daily life?

   How have you experienced the characteristics of this space in your own life or in the lives of those you know and love?

2. *The Peacemaker: Nine.* Summarize the perspective of those in the Nine space. What motivates them the most?

What are the particular temptations of the false self for those in this space?

Define the grace offered to those in this space. What might that grace look like as it is lived out in daily life?

How have you experienced the characteristics of this space in your own life or in the lives of those you know and love?

3. *The Perfectionist: One.* Summarize the perspective of those in the One space. What motivates them the most?

What are the particular temptations of the false self for those in this space?

Define the grace offered to those in this space. What might that grace look like as it is lived out in daily life?

How have you experienced the characteristics of this space in your own life or in the lives of those you know and love?

A Personal Meditation
Facing Criticism: Mark 14:3-9

While he was in Bethany, reclining at the table in the home of Simon the Leper, a woman came with an alabaster jar of very expensive perfume, made of pure nard. She broke the jar and poured the perfume on his head.

Some of those present were saying indignantly to one another, "Why this waste of perfume? It could have been sold for more than a year's wages and the money given to the poor." And they rebuked her harshly.

"Leave her alone," said Jesus. "Why are you bothering her? She has done a beautiful thing to me. The poor you will always have with you, and you can help them any time you want. But you will not always have me. She did what she could. She poured perfume on my body beforehand to prepare for my burial. Truly I tell you, wherever the gospel is preached throughout the world, what she has done will also be told, in memory of her."

1. Take some time to be quiet, and imagine how you would have felt if you had been the woman who came to pour the perfume on Jesus. What feelings might you have had as you entered the room to give your gift to Jesus?

2. How do you feel when you do something you believe is a very good thing and then someone criticizes you for it? How would you feel if someone said you were "wasteful"? How do your feelings about being criticized reflect inclinations of your Enneagram space or triad?

3. How do you criticize yourself? Do your inner criticisms or those of other people shout the loudest in your heart? How did Jesus defend the woman? How might Jesus defend you when you are criticized unjustly?

4. Is there any area of your life today where you are facing criticism? Jesus said the Holy Spirit is our Advocate/Comforter. How might you experience the comfort or advocacy of God today?

7

Looking for Your
Home Space

S o how do we learn our number? This is another great puzzle. There are many online tests and in-book inventories, but often they give suspicious results. This is because it is so very difficult to uncover our blind spots. We respond to inventories with what we know about ourselves, which is often an incomplete picture. The

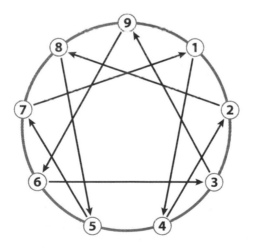

Figure 6. The spaces of the Enneagram

Enneagram describes motivation rather than behavior, and most tests ask about behavior, or our answers reflect our behavior. Another disappointment with the inventories is that they give us permission to circumvent the process. If an inventory quickly gives me my number, I miss the benefits of self-awareness that come from deeper exploration of the Enneagram. That exploration is what this book is about. The more we learn about ourselves from the process of looking for our own space, the deeper our experience on the spiritual journey.

As happy as inventories might be to tell you your number, most of them require a good deal of self-awareness, something our false self does not want us to have. I'd like to suggest that instead of turning to inventories, you spend some time in quiet reflection, thinking about yourself and what you've learned about the Enneagram. Look for places where you already see yourself. Notice where there are clusters of truths about who you are. Be patient with the process. In fact, you might consider this "dating the Enneagram." You do not need to "marry" the first space that you think might work for you. Try it on. Live with it for a while. But let go of it if it doesn't fit. Remember that the Enneagram is supposed to reflect who you are, not dictate who you are. The Enneagram gives words to describe things you may intuitively know about yourself but may have pushed into the background.

As you try to zero in on your number, review the descriptions of the spaces in this book and in two or three other books about the Enneagram. Find brief lists with descriptions of the nine spaces (available on the Internet, or make your own), and ask someone who knows you well to make a wise guess as to your space. If you do choose to do an inventory, go over it carefully with a safe person who loves you. Discuss what you agree with in the inventory and what confuses you. Go to workshops where you can hear others describe their spaces, and notice where you identify with them and where you don't.

Pick the number you think you are, and live with it for several weeks. During that time it will be especially helpful to notice what happens to you when you are under stress. See if that fits the pattern of the number you have picked. Some people discover their number right away. Other people need longer—but they learn a lot about themselves in the process.

TAKE YOUR TIME

I have a good friend who took a year to find her home space. She loved the Enneagram, but she couldn't decide where she landed in the diagram. At first she thought she was a Two. Then she decided she was a One. But at work she definitely acted like a Three. And she did like to learn. Perhaps she was a Five. At last, after a year of working with the Enneagram, she realized that she is a Four. The search might have been shorter with an inventory, but my friend will tell you the process was worth the wait. And, she says, it was probably more accurate. She learned much about herself as she explored each possible space, and when she landed in her home space, it was life giving.

Before I went to my first Enneagram conference, I never would have guessed I am a Four. But in contrast to my friend, I found my home space almost immediately in the presentation at the workshop. (In the dating game, that is like love at first sight. It doesn't happen very often.) I missed the benefit of the process, but I was so intrigued by the accuracy of my home space that I went on to explore the whole diagram, looking for places that taught me about my gifts and my blind spots.

SPIRITUAL DIRECTION

Another good way to find your Enneagram space is with the help of a spiritual director. Spiritual direction is a relationship where one person (the director) listens as a companion to another (the directee) as he or she seeks the direction of God. Spiritual directors receive extensive training and are skilled in listening with love. The spiritual direction relationship is one where we can explore the possibilities of things we cannot see on our own and we can listen to God's invitations to truth.

The Enneagram has become an increasingly helpful tool for spiritual directors as they sit with others. In my own ministry of spiritual direction I find again and again that I go to the insights of the Enneagram. It is not that the Enneagram gives me "answers." It is more that the Enneagram helps me ask questions that open up ways for the person I am meeting with to see their blind spots and to experience renewed freedom.

FIRST STEPS TOWARD YOUR HOME SPACE

If you are not sure of your home space and you would like to ponder the Enneagram a bit more, the following suggestions (a summary of this chapter) may be helpful.

1. A good place to start is to read through the descriptions of all the spaces in chapters four, five, and six. Notice anything that reminds you of yourself. Underline or highlight those statements, or make your own list of these characteristics, noting the space number where you found each one.

2. Spend some time thinking about the spaces where you see clusters of characteristics that seem to describe you. Look more closely at the descriptions of those spaces. What seems to fit for you in each space? What does not fit?

3. Ask someone who knows and loves you well to look at your lists and mark the ones that seem to most clearly reflect you. Discuss your own conclusions with this person.

4. Remembering how you behave when you are stressed may reveal some hidden motivations. When you are under stress, what adjectives best describe how you feel and how you act? In which spaces do you see those negative characteristics?

5. What space would you most like to be in? Why? Which space would you least like to be in? Why?

6. What are some of your own motivations that are least attractive to you? And what are some of your own motivations that seem to reflect your gifts?

7. Spend some time in quiet musing about what you have learned about yourself. Ask the Holy Spirit to reveal more to you.

8. Pick a space that seems most likely to be your home space. Live with this for three or four weeks, paying special attention to how you are when you are using your gifts and how you are when you are under stress. Then spend some time reflecting back on these weeks and see whether you sense you have found you home space. If not, try again!

FOR REFLECTION AND DISCUSSION

If you have been meeting with a small group to discuss this book, now is a good time for participants to share from their own engagement with the Enneagram. The following questions will help people do that. If you are reading this book on your own, think of a trusted friend you might dialogue with about your own journey.

1. What have you learned about yourself from the Enneagram that surprises you?

2. What thoughts do you have at this point in the journey about what might be your home space?

3. Do others (allow group feedback here) feel that you have made an accurate choice? In what ways do they think your choice fits the way they have experienced you? In what ways might it not fit?

4. What do you like and what do you not like about the home space you have chosen?

5. How do you want to continue the journey of the Enneagram?

A Personal Meditation
Clay Jars: 2 Corinthians 4:7-10

But we have this treasure in jars of clay to show that this all-surpassing power is from God and not from us. We are hard pressed on every side, but not crushed; perplexed, but not in despair; persecuted, but not abandoned; struck down, but not destroyed. We always carry around in our body the death of Jesus, so that the life of Jesus may also be revealed in our body.

As you look for your home space, you may find yourself disappointed with what you are learning about yourself. Paul's image of clay jars may help.

1. Picture a clay jar or another container that is not very impressive. Next to it, picture an artistic, beautiful container that might be kept with the fine china. What image comes to mind that describes how you view yourself?

2. What does the Enneagram say about how you are "a clay jar"? What do you think about Paul's observation that this keeps the focus on God and not on us? Do you agree with that? Do you like it?

3. What words describe how you feel when you come face to face with your limitations, when you wish you were more than just a clay jar? Do you feel hard pressed, perplexed, persecuted, knocked down, or something else?

4. "Through suffering, our bodies continue to share in the death of Jesus so that the life of Jesus may also be seen in our bodies" (2 Corinthians 4:10 NLT). Paul was probably talking about physical persecution. But we can also experience inner struggles as we seek to follow Jesus. Think of a time when you have suffered from giving in to your Enneagram compulsions. How was grace revealed to you or to others in this experience?

5. What is the invitation of God to you in this passage?

8

Understanding the Wings
and the Arrows

I have a good friend who is at home in the Two space. He is one of the most loving, giving people I know. But over the years we've been friends, I have seen again and again how he is prone to join groups and churches with high hopes of positive engagement, only to become so distressed that he leaves in anger. Another friend, a Five, is not only full of wisdom, she is also disciplined and intentional about how she lives her life. It is surprising, then, that she often finds herself binge watching television with a bowl of ice cream next to the popcorn. How do my two friends end up acting in ways that so contradict their best gifts?

My friends are not alone in the bewilderment they feel about their unexpected behavior. Even the apostle Paul said, "I have discovered this principle of life—that when I want to do what is right, I inevitably do what is wrong. I love God's law with all my heart. But there is another power within me that is at war with my mind. . . . Oh, what a miserable person I am!" (Romans 7:21-24 NLT). What, we might ask, does the Enneagram have to say about *that*?

This brings us to the wings and the arrows of the Enneagram. But first a word of warning: the wings and arrows may not be for beginners. This is a deeper level of the Enneagram. When I teach Enneagram workshops, the wings and arrows are part of the advanced workshop. One problem is that the theory of the wings and the arrows may complicate things for people still looking for their home space. A riskier problem is that the wings and arrows may tempt beginners to "self-management." If, for instance, I don't like the compulsions of my home space, I may think I can just suck it up and move to a wing or an arrow space and live happily ever after. But it's not that simple.

That said, the perspective of wings and arrows rounds out the stance of our home space in very helpful ways. The wings and the arrows give words to aspects of our view of life that are not front and center in our home space. This means that as we understand our wings and arrow spaces, we grow in self-awareness. And understanding the wings and arrows gives words to aspects of transformation we may be longing for.

HEART TRIAD	
Two Wings ⟶	One and Three
Three Wings ⟶	Two and Four
Four Wings ⟶	Three and Five
HEAD TRIAD	
Five Wings ⟶	Four and Six
Six Wings ⟶	Five and Seven
Seven Wings ⟶	Six and Eight
GUT TRIAD	
Eight Wings ⟶	Seven and Nine
Nine Wings ⟶	Eight and One
One Wings ⟶	Nine and Two

Figure 7. The wings

THE WINGS OF THE ENNEAGRAM

The wings, in Enneagram terminology, are the spaces on each side of your home space. So the wings of the One are Nine and Two. The wings of the Two are One and Three—and so on around the diagram. Loretta Brady says she likes to think of the wings as neighbors. "I don't 'live' in the houses on either side of me," she says. "But they are very familiar to me. Sometimes I visit there for a while." If she knows her neighbors well she may even act like she lives there while she visits.

Another way to think of the wings is to picture a rainbow. The colors all flow together. But a child drawing a rainbow would probably draw an arch with the red crayon, followed by an arch with the blue crayon, then maybe a yellow crayon, and, if he is very creative, even a purple crayon. That is not what a real rainbow looks like. It is also the mistake a beginner might make on the Enneagram journey, thinking that the spaces are rigid lines and using the Enneagram to put people in boxes. Reality is much more fluid. Just as the colors of a rainbow flow into each other, the spaces of the Enneagram flow from one to the next. A person in the Five space, for instance, will always love to gather information and wisdom. But for a time he may "visit" the Six space and be very aware and even fearful of the influence of authority and the perceived rules of life. Or he may "visit" the Four space and live with the melancholy that comes from focusing on what's missing in life.

Some Enneagram writers teach that each space has a dominant wing. Other Enneagram teachers believe that each space is influenced by both wings. Some people say that we are influenced by one wing in some circumstances and the other wing in other circumstances. It is also possible that one wing is more dominant in one season of life and the other wing more of an influence in the next season of life. In whatever way the influence of your wings shows up, it will be helpful to spend some time looking at both of those spaces. This gives you two more space descriptions to help identify perspectives on your way of living life that were hidden to you before.

A good friend of mine is a One. She is at home in the One space, even though she is sometimes frustrated when she sees the compulsions of that space played out in her own life. She is also aware of her Two wing. She is delighted with the pleasure she has in helping out in her church in ways that reflect the Two perspective. She is involved in worship, in prayer ministry, and in hospitality.

Then she bumped into an issue that stumped her. She simply could not make a decision that needed to be made. She was stuck in a malaise resulting from her indecision. Because we are good friends, and because we both talk the language of the Enneagram, I felt free to ask if her indecision was coming from her Nine wing. She lit up. "That's it. My Nine wing is holding me back from doing something about this!" She looked back over the perspective of the Nine space and was able to move ahead as she embraced its compulsions and gifts.

Another way the wing spaces may be helpful is for people who are torn between two spaces in determining their home space. If these two spaces are separated by one space, that space may indicate the home space. This can be especially helpful if the person is resistant to the characteristics of his or her home space. ("I don't want to be like my mother!" Or "That's my boss, and I am definitely not like that!") The Enneagram uncovers our blind spots in ways that are sometimes uncomfortable. Embracing the truths of our home space can be life changing, and our wings may help us identify that space.

We can also benefit from the wings by being intentional about looking at the gifts of our wing spaces. A Three, for instance, may try to be more aware of the importance of authenticity of the Four space. This is helpful when the Three person is tempted to fall into the compulsion of deceit and self-aggrandizement. Or the Six might choose to let go of the restraints of authority and join in the fun recommended by the Seven wing. Wings, in some sense, can help us fly away from our home space, at least for a short time.

One more source of information from the wings comes from the triad each wing is in. If a wing is not in your home triad, you may gain insight into yourself by looking at the characteristics of the triad that wing is in. Anything that helps us understand why we do what we do is worth pursuing.

It is important to take in all of these possibilities from the wing spaces and digest them in light of your own life and temperament. With that in mind, here are several questions to help you engage with your wing spaces.

WORKING WITH YOUR WINGS

1. Look at the descriptions of your wing spaces in the previous chapters. Make a list of the characteristics that look most familiar to you in these two spaces.

2. As you muse on your list, what characteristics might provide a healthy balance for you in the tensions of your life right now?

3. What aspects of your wings spaces are not life giving for you in this season of life?

THE ARROWS OF THE ENNEAGRAM

The arrows of the Enneagram can be a bit confusing, but exploring them is well worth the effort. It will help to keep the Enneagram diagram in mind as we look at another layer of this amazing paradigm.

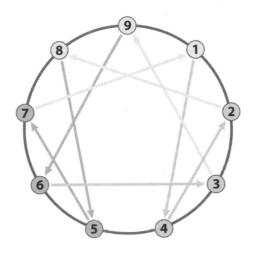

Figure 8. The arrows

To get started, look at your number on the diagram. Notice the arrow pointing away from your number. What number does it point to? And now look at the arrow pointing to your number. Where does it originate? These two spaces connected to your home space by arrows are the ones we will be talking about.

Most Enneagram teachers use the words *consolation* and *desolation* to describe the insights the arrows give to us. According to classic Enneagram theory, the arrow pointing *away* from your number is the direction we move when we are under stress or living in unhealthy ways. This arrow points to a place of desolation for us. *Desolation* is an ancient word describing how we feel when we are sad, unhappy, and distressed. In contrast, the arrow pointing to your space originates at the space that describes how we are living when we are in a healthy place in our lives. This space is a place of consolation, or comfort, help and support. It may help to think that when we are under stress, we are tempted to take the "easy" way out—to slide with the arrow to an unhealthy place. But when we are more self-aware and intentional, we may choose to intentionally go against the arrow (and swim upstream) to the space that will help us find relief.

Let me describe what that might look like for the Four, the space I am most familiar with. When I am living contentedly in my own space, I am living with opportunities to be creative—with words, visually, and in relationships. I am involved in friendships where I can authentically be myself. I am content to be who I am and not who I am not. I do not constantly compare myself with other people, take things personally, and believe that I am missing out on things that everyone else has. (Living in deep contentment happens occasionally and often lasts for about a minute or two.) When I am stressed by deadlines, difficult relationships, or my chronic self-doubt, I *slide* into the Two space. I do not feel close to God when I am under stress, so I rev things up to try to connect with other people. Unfortunately, I do this by taking responsibility for other people's emotions and thinking that I know what is best for those I love. I succumb to the lie of my Four false self that I am inferior and missing out in life. I have to do all I can to correct that image. So I begin to act in the negative ways that tempt people in the Two space. I can manipulate and control, all in the name of love. This, of course, doesn't work, but I'm still learning that.

The arrows suggest why my Two friend often walks out of relationships in anger and why my Five friend unwisely over-indulges in television and food. Under stress, both friends are sliding down the slippery slope of their arrows to places that are not healthy for them. The Two friend slides into the control and anger of an unhealthy Eight. My Five friend slides into the gluttony of an unhealthy Seven. To find relief from these unhealthy places, they can both look to the spaces pointing to their own spaces and experiment with the perspective of those other spaces. For the Two this would be the Four space, and for the Five this would be the Eight space. Moving toward the arrow of consolation is, of course, much easier said than done.

If I have a moment of self-awareness in the midst of the stress, as a Four I can choose to move against my arrow to the qualities of the One space. Serenity is the grace given to those in the One space—the ability to respond to life without reactivity. When I remember that, and when I catch myself in reactivity, I can sometimes take a deep breath and stop reacting out of my own self-doubt, which tells me that whatever the mess is, it is all my fault. I can question my thoughts that other people have it better than me. I can let go of my sense of the way things should be and accept the way they are. In all honesty, this way of thinking usually feels very strange to me. But sometimes, if the moment of consolation extends into several minutes, I can experience the serenity of letting go of my desire that things be absolutely perfect, according to my particular standards.

Let me give another example. I had an email exchange with a Six friend who was bemoaning her exaggerated sense of responsibility, compulsion to get things done, and desire for control. I mentioned to her that some of that may come from the influence of her Three arrow. When a Six is under stress, the temptation is to slide into the Three space, in which accomplishments, looking good to other people, and finishing the task would all be very important "Whoa," she said. "That slices pretty close to home! Going to the Three space is so enticing." I wrote back that, in contrast, listening to the perspective of the Nine space may help Sixes to go with the flow and be more relaxed about life. Our email exchange was an Enneagram moment.

The arrows do not mean that we change types. We do not become another type when we are very stressed or very relaxed. But we do pick up some characteristics of our arrow types, and knowing what those characteristics are will enrich our self-awareness.

CHECKING OUT YOUR ARROWS

Before we nuance the theory of the Enneagram arrows even more, take a few minutes to look closely at your own arrows. Notice how one is most likely to bring you consolation, health, and support, and the other is most likely to lead you to a place of desolation or despair.

1. My arrow of desolation (the one that points away from my number to another number) is number _____.

   Look back in the book at the description of this number. Make a list of the characteristics in that space that might lead you into deeper stress.

2. My arrow of consolation (the one that points from another number to my number) is number _____.

   Look back in the book at the description of this number. Make a list of the characteristics in that space that might lead you out of stress.

3. Now complete the following sentences:

   When I am content to be in my home space, I _____

   _____

   When I slide into the negative characteristics of the space my arrow points to, I _____

   _____

   _____

   When I choose to try on the positive characteristics of the space my arrow points from, I _____

   _____

   _____

A SECOND LOOK AT THE ARROWS

Now that we've established that the arrows point away from a place of integration and consolation for us and toward a place of disintegration and desolation, I'd like to suggest that you go back and revisit both of your arrow spaces. It would be a mistake to think that one space is all bad and the other is all good. Life is too complicated for that.

Enneagram teachers often point out that buried in both spaces are good characteristics as well as negative characteristics. Remember that Jesus called Satan the great deceiver. Any lie will do. Our blind spots work well in any space. This means that even though the classic, most likely pattern of our arrow will be true most of the time, there may be characteristics of both spaces that invite us to unexpected conclusions. This would explain why I struggle with perfectionism, even though the One space is supposed to be good for me. And this may be why I can be very loving and helpful to people in need, even though the Two space describes many temptations for me. Looking for the truths buried in my arrow spaces has been helpful to me.

Take a moment to look at your negative arrow space, the one pointing away from your home space. What characteristics in that space seem to be life giving for you, even though they may be buried in characteristics that tempt you in unhealthy ways? Now look at your positive arrow space, the one that points to your home space. What characteristics of that space look more like compulsions than gifts to you?

Consider how this might play out for the Two and Eight spaces, which are connected by an arrow. For the Two person, the classic theory would say that in stress he or she would pick up the negatives of the Eight space. And indeed the most likely scenario is that a Two in stress will become manipulative and controlling. But a Two person also reflects the dynamic leadership of the Eight.

Given the opportunity, a Two can lead a team, a family, or a church committee in ways that enhance their ability to love and help those they influence.

Eights, in their passion for social justice, have done wonders in helping people in need around the world. At their best, Eights use their power to love others, reflecting the Two space. But Eights can also pick up some of the negatives of the Two space by hiding their own needs from themselves and others, meddling, and pushing their own agenda. While the classic theory of the arrows probably describes the most likely experience of Twos and Eights, people in both spaces can benefit from rounding out their perspectives to notice both the positives and the negatives of the other space.

TOO MANY SPACES?

I will say that all of this can be irritating. It was for me. *Why*, I wondered, *is the Enneagram any good if we add up the home space, the wings, and the arrows and find ourselves in five of the nine spaces?* This is not a great statistic. But even though I learn the most from my home space, I have come to value all five of the spaces that speak into my life. In fact, it makes the Enneagram seem even more authentic to me. I do not fit neatly into one little space. I spill over into others. And each one tells me something about myself, something I need to know in order to grow.

It helps me to remember that the Enneagram is like a mirror for me. It reflects who I am, warts and all. I am reminded of the three-way mirror on my dresser when I was growing up. I loved to move the two mirrors on the side of the main one so I could see many images, reflected down the line. The Enneagram also does that for me. I see the main reflection in my home space and then I see many more reflections as I "turn" the diagram and look through other spaces.

The goal here is not to admire all those images, even though I liked doing that as a little girl. The goal is to grow in self-awareness so that we can come to God with all that is good and with all that we don't like about ourselves. In God's presence we receive grace.

God gives us grace, whatever space is influencing us. In fact, we don't even need to figure out the arrows to experience God's grace. The arrows may be helpful, but if they are not, leave them for a while. The truth is that God is always waiting to be gracious to us and always ready to extend mercy (Isaiah 30:18). Knowledge of the Enneagram, even with its complicated arrows, reminds us that we need that grace.

If the arrows intrigue you, spend some time with these questions and see what you learn.

ANOTHER LOOK AT THE ARROWS

1. Look back at your arrow spaces and add to your lists of what influences you in stress and in contentment. Add the positive characteristics from the space that often brings you desolation and the negative characteristics from the space that usually brings you consolation.

2. Think of a current situation that is very stressful for you. Look over your lists. Mark the descriptions that best describe how you honestly see yourself in this situation. What do you learn about yourself as you muse over these lists?

3. Think of a time in your life when you felt content and at peace with yourself. Again, looking at your lists, notice what descriptions best fit your times of contentment.

FOR REFLECTION AND DISCUSSION

If you know your home space, spend some time reflecting on how the wings and arrows influence your life and relationships.

1. What are your *wing* spaces?

   What additional information do the descriptions of these spaces give to you to help increase your self-awareness?

   What questions would you like to ask those whose home space is one of your wing spaces about living in that space?

2. What is your *arrow of desolation* or disintegration—where you are likely to go when you are under stress?

   What characteristics of that space do you see in your own life when you are stressed out? How do you feel about those characteristics?

   What would you like to ask those whose home space is your space of desolation?

3. What is your *arrow of consolation* or integration—where you might go for help when you are feeling compulsive about your gifts?

   What characteristics of that space look like they might be helpful to you?

   When have you intentionally picked up one of those characteristics? What was that like for you?

   What questions would you like to ask of those whose home space is your space of consolation?

4. What is your impression of the wings and the arrows? Are they helpful to you? How do they round out your understanding of the Enneagram?

A *Personal* Meditation
The Grace of Quietness and Rest: Isaiah 30:15-16, 18

For thus said the Lord GOD, *the Holy One of Israel:*
In returning and rest you shall be saved;
    in quietness and in trust shall be your strength.
But you refused and said,
"No! We will flee upon horses." . . .
Therefore the LORD *waits to be gracious to you;*
    therefore he will rise up to show mercy to you. (NRSV)

Take several deep breaths and relax your body as you wait for your mind and heart to settle. Let your mind and heart wander slowly through the following questions.

1. Think of an area of your life where you would like to experience rest, quietness, and trust. Now be honest with yourself and think of how you might be refusing God's salvation for you in this situation. In what ways might you be saying, "No, I'll try to do such and such first." How do your alternative plans reflect your arrow space of desolation?

2. Consider the possibility of finding strength in quietness and confidence. What is it like for you to be quiet? What is it like for you when you trust God? If you were to embrace some of the perspectives of your arrow space of consolation, in what ways do you think you might feel more quietness and trust?

3. Spend some time with the truths that "God waits to be gracious to you" and "God will rise up to show mercy to you." Write these truths in your own words.

4. Reread the verses from Isaiah. What word or phrase stands out to you? Do you sense an invitation from God for you today?

9

Biblical Truths Reflected in the Enneagram

For many Christians one of the first questions that comes to mind after they encounter the Enneagram is, How does all of this intersect with the Bible? Is the Enneagram perspective biblical? Where in Scripture do we find the same truths we see in the Enneagram?

The Bible does not talk about the Enneagram, but the teaching of the Enneagram reflects the truths of Scripture. What we see in the Enneagram is like looking through another window into the underlying assumptions of the Bible. We see the same truths in different words.

STARTING AT THE BEGINNING

In the book of Genesis we learn about the creation of men and women. After God created the sky and the earth, light and darkness, water and land, animals and plants, God created men and women in God's own image. This means that at our best we look like God. God was pleased. It was all "very good" (Genesis 1:31). Likewise, the Enneagram also starts with what is good about us. We are all created with good gifts. And at that first workshop I went to, I noticed right away that the gifts identified by the Enneagram reflect the fruits of the Holy Spirit, identified by the apostle Paul in his letter to the Galatians: love, joy, peace, patience, kindness, goodness, faithfulness, gentleness, and self-control (Galatians 5:22-23). The lists do not match up exactly, but the similarity amazed me. As a Christian, it is not a huge leap for me to see that the Enneagram identifies gifts that remind me we are created in the image of God and that the Holy Spirit bears fruit in my life.

Both the Bible and the Enneagram also describe the downhill slope human beings take. In the first chapter of Genesis, God saw that all of creation was "good." By the third chapter the human part of creation did not look so good anymore. And soon into that first workshop I attended about the Enneagram, things for us didn't look so good either. Just as I had seen the fruits of the Spirit in the gifts identified in the Enneagram, I saw the traditional seven deadly sins in the passions or compulsions identified by the Enneagram: anger, greed, sloth, pride, lust, envy, and gluttony. Again, not an exact list, but very similar.

So the Enneagram confirms what the Bible says: the good news that we are created in the image of God has become the bad news that we have tarnished that image. (And, as we'll see, the Enneagram also confirms that grace is the good news that provides a way out of the bad news.)

THE FIRST BIG MISTAKE

From the very beginning Adam and Eve got it wrong. God had given them everything they needed. But they wanted more. They were allowed to eat from almost every tree in the garden. The trees were "pleasing to the eye and good for food" (Genesis 2:9). Sounds like a perfect arrangement. But there was one thing—there was a tree in the middle of the garden that was off limits. The tree of the knowledge of good and evil. "When you eat from it," God said, "you will certainly die" (Genesis 2:17).

You know what happened. The serpent came along and asked, "Did God really say, 'You must not eat from any tree in the garden'?" (Genesis 3:1). Interestingly, when Eve answered the question, she made God's command even more stringent. She said, "We may eat fruit from the trees in the garden, but God did say, 'You must not eat fruit from the tree that is in the middle of the garden, and you must not touch it, or you will die'" (Genesis 3:2-3). God had not said anything about touching the tree. The false, ego-centered self showed itself right away when Eve made God's word more difficult than it was.

But then the serpent came in for the kill as he blatantly contradicted God. "You will not certainly die," he said, "for God knows that when you eat from it your eyes will be opened, and you will be like God, knowing good and evil" (Genesis 3:4-5). We deal with echoes of that first temptation every day. "Did God really say . . . ? This cannot be true." We do this with our conscious and unconscious questions: Did God really say that I am loved as I am? Did God really say that I am enough as I am? Isn't there something more I am supposed to do or not do?

We follow in the footsteps of Adam and Eve and eat from that forbidden tree when we believe that how God has made us and what God has given us is not enough. Commentators tell us that the tree in the middle of the garden is a symbol of human limitations that are part of creation. We cannot be everything to everyone. We cannot even be all we want to be for ourselves. Our limitations bring us to God. From the very beginning God built into our humanity something that would remind us that God is God and we are not.

HERE COMES THE JUDGE

The name of the tree explains another reason why it is forbidden. Eating from that tree not only affects how we view ourselves, it affects how we view others. We want to know the difference between good and evil not because we want to love better. We are already able to love because we are created in God's image and have gifts that express God's love to share with others. The problem is that we want the knowledge of good and evil because we want to judge ourselves and others. We want our eyes to be opened in order to see what God sees because we want to be God.

In his book *Repenting of Religion*, Greg Boyd has this to say:

> We are not satisfied being God-like in our capacity to love; we also want to become God-like in our capacity to judge—to determine what is good and what is evil. When we do that, we lose the capacity to love—unlike God, we cannot judge and love at the same time. The essence of sin is that we play God. . . . We critically assess and evaluate everything and everyone from our limited, finite, biased perspective.

Boyd's book is not about the Enneagram, but the connection is clear. In the Enneagram, we see nine ways we judge. We judge, heaven forbid, according to our own giftedness. First of all, we judge ourselves. If, for example, success is good, then we judge ourselves for perceived failure. If peace is good, we judge ourselves for anything that leads us into conflict. If we have the gift of power and leadership, then all weakness in ourselves is unacceptable. If we believe in joy and are joyful most of the time, then pain is something to avoid at all costs. When we live like this, whatever space we are in, we focus our attention and energy on avoiding what we judge to be wrong. We assume God cannot love us if we miss the mark in our giftedness. First we condemn ourselves. Then we judge others. We cannot, as Boyd says, love and judge at the same time.

JESUS WARNS ABOUT JUDGING

Jesus had something to say about judging: "Do not judge, or you too will be judged. For in the same way you judge others, you will be judged, and with the measure you use, it will be measured to you" (Matthew 7:1-2). Eugene Peterson translates Jesus' words about judgment this way: "That critical spirit has a way of boomeranging" (Matthew 7:2 *The Message*). The Enneagram says the same thing, in different words.

Here is the way we play the boomerang game, Enneagram version. We judge ourselves because we do not express our giftedness as we think we should. Then we think others are judging us by those same standards. This makes us mad, so we judge others for judging us. This leads us to judge others the way we judge ourselves, for not exhibiting the "standards" of our gifts. First one to the judgment seat wins.

We all judge ourselves and others in ways that are unique to the style of our false self. The Enneagram can help us put words to how we do this. Listen to how judgment might play out in the three triads. Someone in the heart triad believes she needs to fix everyone's problems. A dear friend has the flu. The heart triad person "knows" that she "should" take her friend to the doctor, bring her soup later that day, and pray without ceasing for her health. But this is a busy week. After all, she is responsible for lots of other things too. She begins to feel inadequate. *I can't do all I am supposed to do! What's wrong with me? Why can't I push just a little harder? I am so defective.* About ten seconds after judging herself for being defective, this heart triad person changes her tune. *Why can't my friend take better care of herself? She never should have gone out last night when it was obvious that she was coming down with the flu. Why does she expect me to do all of this? What's wrong with her?*

Or consider how someone in the head triad might experience ten-second judgment. This person is teaching an adult Sunday school with a friend in church. The friend suggests that they sit in a circle and "share" instead of listening to a lecture. Hmmm. *Not a good idea*, says the head triad person. *That would be a waste of time, sharing ignorance. Besides, I'm not very good at sharing my feelings. I'm better at teaching and sharing all I've been learning. But no one wants to hear about all the thinking I've done for this class. Why is everybody in this church so wishy-washy? Why don't they want to hear what I have to say?*

Or the person in the gut triad: her company has just been reorganized. Ha! What a joke. She could have told them months ago that this wouldn't work. Her new boss wants her to bring more clients to the company. But she's not good at schmoozing. She just can't kiss up to people. But then nobody listens to her anyway. They are all jerks. (That only took about eight seconds.)

In each of these examples, we can see that whatever we value (in these scenarios, helping people, teaching people, influencing people) becomes a standard for our lives. When we fail to meet the standard, we blame and judge others. Even Adam, in that account of the first sin, blamed Eve. "She made me do it," he told God. Then Eve blamed the serpent. God didn't buy it.

Adam and Eve's experience is like a foretaste of what we do in our Enneagram spaces. The gifts God has given us are all that we need to love others, serve God, and enjoy life. But we want more. When we are under stress, we are ripe for temptation. We rush to exaggerate our gifts and judge ourselves and others for falling short. We are no longer satisfied with what God has given us. We are no longer satisfied with being good. We want to be perfect. We are no longer satisfied with being successful. We simply cannot fail. Or we are no longer satisfied with being an influential leader. We must be in charge. When we are exaggerating our gifts, we are saying that we know what is good for us and for everyone else. And we know what is evil. Let us be the judge.

HIDE AND SEEK

Back to the story of Adam and Eve. We know what happened next. After Adam and Eve did exactly what God had told them not to do, they ran into the bushes to hide (Genesis 3:8). We do not need to go into the bushes. We have a much more interesting place to hide: behind our giftedness. When we follow the path of disintegration observed in the Enneagram, we begin to exaggerate our giftedness and overplay our gifts so we can hide behind them. If I act in very, very peaceful ways and don't ruffle any feathers, says the Nine, maybe no one will get mad at me or disagree with me. If I make a lot of suggestions and am really helpful, says the Two, maybe people will think I am as wonderful as I think I am. If I do everything the boss (or Mom or Dad) asks, says the Six, maybe I won't be so fearful. Whatever our Enneagram space, we do what Adam and Eve did. We hide.

THE MASQUERADE

But grace was there from the beginning. God found Adam and Eve and "made garments of skin for Adam and his wife and clothed them" (Genesis 3:21). But when we are living compulsively, we are wearing "garments" that we have fashioned for ourselves, garments made out of our gifts. We dress ourselves to look like the people we wish we were. We take the gifts given to us and use them for our own purposes.

This is really quite ingenious. We have come to believe the lies that what God gave me is not enough, that I am not enough, and that if I want to be a better person, I need to polish up my gifts and impress others with their glitter. In my inner being, I want to be like Jesus. But instead I dress up and masquerade as someone who is always good, helpful, successful, creative, wise, loyal, joyful, powerful, or peaceful. When we are expressing these gifts as a reflection of God's love, we offer them freely. When we believe we always have to be known for how wonderful our gifts are, then we exaggerate the gifts and reflect the egotistical, prideful false self.

Since I am a Four, perhaps I can poke some fun here. The Four person wants to be special, look special, and contribute something special to society. And we do that, in artistic, creative ways. But what do Fours do when they fear they are not as unique as they'd like to be? We do what people in all of the spaces do. We try to look good. For Fours one of the more benign expressions of this masquerade may be quite literally in our physical appearance. At one Enneagram conference I attended, a woman waltzed in late sporting a large, pink fur boa scarf over her shoulder. I thought to myself, *Oh, good, there's another Four here.* (I was right.)

But the masquerade takes a darker form for Fours when we exaggerate our desire to be special to the point that we think no one can really understand us. We are that unique. We spiral down into the place where all we can see is that we are completely different from other people. The next step is to believe we are missing what everyone else has. After we judge ourselves for our inadequacy, we hide once again by trying to be different, trying to be special, and trying to be noticed.

Am I being unkind to Fours here? If so, it is only because I see this in the mirror every day. And I know that every space has its own masquerade. In fact, if you doubt this, here would be a good place to stop and ask yourself, *Where do I pretend? Where do I exaggerate who I am? Where do I lay it on with my gifts in the hopes that people will notice me, respect me, and love me?* We all have our own forms of the masquerade. The Enneagram tells us where to look.

A NEW TESTAMENT REFLECTION OF THE DILEMMA

This gets very complicated. How do we know when we are exaggerating our gifts? How do we know when we are judging others? How do we stop doing what we don't want to do?

The apostle Paul described his experience of our dilemma in his letter to the church in Rome:

> I need something *more*! For if I know the law but still can't keep it, and if the power of sin within me keeps sabotaging my best intentions, I obviously need help! I realize that I don't have what it takes. I can will it, but I can't *do* it. I decide to do good, but I don't *really* do it; I decide not to do bad, but then I do it anyway. My decisions, such as they are, don't result in actions. Something has gone wrong deep within me and gets the better of me every time. (Romans 7:17-20 *The Message*)

Paul described his own dilemma in terms of the law and sinfulness. The Enneagram uses different words to describe how we sabotage our desire to follow Jesus. We have taught ourselves, according to the gifts of our Enneagram space, that there is one way to obey God. We have taught ourselves that our gifts are the most important thing about us and that if we don't express our gifts well, we will disappoint God, others, and ourselves. Disaster, we fear, is just around the corner. So we up the ante, rev up our gifts, and become obsessed with ourselves. "Something," says Paul, "has gone wrong deep within me and gets the better of me every time."

A person in the One space might say it this way: I really want to be a good person. But it makes me so mad when I can't do that. And when I think other people aren't carrying their weight in doing things right, well, that makes me really angry. My anger takes over and I end up hurting the people I love.

Or a person in the Three space might say, I really want to be successful in my relationships as well as in my job. We just moved into town. I don't really know anyone. Worse yet, they don't know me. A lady who lives in one of the nicest houses on our street invited me over for drinks on her deck with some other neighbors. I hate things like that. But I didn't want her to think I was antisocial, so I went. Next thing I know, I'm in the neighborhood book club. And I hate to read. Now what do I do? I'm supposed to love my neighbors but this is driving me crazy!

Or listen to a person in the Six space: I like that I am a loyal person. I like trying to do what those I respect what me to do. I always thought God wanted me to be a missionary. But my parents wanted me to go into business. I'm making a lot of money now, but I'm not happy. I don't think I can be a missionary anymore. It scares me to think of doing something new. Besides, the country I wanted to go to has a lot of terrorists. I didn't want to disappoint my parents, but now I'm afraid I'm disappointing God.

In each of these scenarios the person wanted to walk in the way of Jesus. But the perspective of his or her Enneagram space sabotaged that desire. The Enneagram gives words to the particular slant each space brings to difficulties we all face. The Enneagram is like a map on my spiritual journey, leading me to love. I agree with Paul that it is only Christ who can save me from the contradictions in my way of being. In Scripture I learn about the availability of God's love and grace to help me. Through the Enneagram I am given new ways of understanding this important truth.

The Enneagram can be taught from many religious and secular perspectives. But as I bring my own Christian values to Enneagram teaching, I believe that because of the Enneagram, I understand Scripture better, I understand those I love better, and I understand myself better. This is a journey God has invited me to continue.

FOR REFLECTION AND DISCUSSION

1. From what you have learned about the Enneagram, why do you think it is important to start with our giftedness?

2. As you think about the gifts the Creator God has given you, what thoughts and feelings come to mind?

3. "We follow in the footsteps of Adam and Eve and eat from that forbidden tree when we believe that how God has made us and what God has given us is not enough. . . . From the very beginning God built into our humanity something that would remind us that God is God and we are not." How does the Enneagram remind us that God is God and we are not?

4. How are we tempted to judge ourselves and others according to our own giftedness?

   Can you think of a time when you have done that?

5. How might the tendency to judge show up in each triad?

6. "When we follow the path of disintegration observed in the Enneagram, we begin to exaggerate our giftedness and overplay our gifts so we can hide behind them." What would it be like for you to overplay the gifts given to you?

   What effect does that have on your relationships?

7. "We have taught ourselves, according to the gifts of our Enneagram space, that there is one way to obey God. We have taught ourselves that our gifts are the most important thing about us and that if we don't express our gifts well, we will disappoint God, others, and ourselves. Disaster, we fear, is just around the corner. So we up the ante, rev up our gifts, and become obsessed with ourselves. 'Something,' says Paul, 'has gone wrong deep within me and gets the better of me every time.'" Think of a time recently when you revved up your giftedness. What do you do when you "masquerade"?

   What effect does it have on others and on you?

A Personal Meditation

Jesus' View of Prayer: Matthew 6:5-8

When you pray, don't be like the hypocrites who love to pray publicly on street corners and in the synagogues where everyone can see them. I tell you the truth, that is all the reward they will ever get. But when you pray, go away by yourself, shut the door behind you, and pray to your Father in private. Then your Father, who sees everything, will reward you.

When you pray, don't babble on and on as the Gentiles do. They think their prayers are answered merely by repeating their words again and again. Don't be like them, for your Father knows exactly what you need even before you ask him! (NLT)

1. Jesus is speaking here of the way we pray. But his words can speak to many areas of our life. In what area of your spiritual life are you most apt to care what other people think of you? What do you do to make them think highly of you? How do you feel about their admiration?

2. What "rewards" do you look for as you express the gifts you have been given?

3. What is your response to Jesus' teaching that we should pray in private? Is praying in private as satisfying for you as praying when someone else can hear you? And what about "babbling"? When are you apt to babble in prayer?

4. Looking back over your answers to these questions, in what ways might your thoughts reflect your Enneagram triad or space?

5. How do you respond to Jesus' teaching that God "knows exactly what you need even before you ask him"? Try to express this truth using the terminology of your Enneagram space.

6. What part of this teaching is most life giving for you today?

10

Addicted to Ourselves

～⌁〜

A t this point on our journey into the Enneagram, many people are inclined to say, "Why does this matter? It's interesting. It's probably a good idea for me to identify my compulsions. And I'm certainly enjoying pointing my finger at others' compulsions. (Not a good idea!) But what difference does all of this make in my relationship with God?"

My own experience with the Enneagram is that it not only speaks to the great puzzle of who I am, it also speaks to the mystery of why I sometimes feel alienated from my Creator God, and why I sometimes alienate myself from those I love. Knowledge of the Enneagram has led me into more authentic self-awareness, more loving relationships with other people, and deeper places in my soul where I can worship God in truth and grace. But this process has often been painful. The only reason I keep going on is that the pain of the intervention of the Enneagram in my life leads to transformation by the grace of God.

HOW DOES TRANSFORMATION HAPPEN?

Transformation is something that happens to us, but it cannot happen without us. God invites us to transformation. He never forces it on us. This means that lasting transformation may not happen until we agree with God that we need transforming grace in our lives. God uses many tools to invite us into transformation: circumstances, other people, personal meditation, Scripture, nature, sermons, service opportunities. The list is endless. Knowledge of the Enneagram is one of these tools. The Enneagram gives us words that help us show up in the presence of God's love and transforming grace.

I have found that the Enneagram respects the observation that the soul is shy, like a wild animal. Parker Palmer says that "if we want to see a wild animal, the last thing we should do is to go crashing through the woods, shouting for it to come out." Instead, we need to "walk quietly into the woods and sit silently" until "out of the corner of an eye we will catch a glimpse of the precious wildness we seek." Palmer is not writing about the Enneagram, but this is a good reminder that we dare not crash through the woods of the Enneagram yelling for our soul to come out. The Enneagram is much more likely to give us "glimpses" into our souls. The process may be painful, but it is gentle.

When our family drove through Yellowstone National Park several years ago, my husband was very eager to see wild animals. Sometimes there were signs to help us: "Buffalo crossing. Stay in car." My husband, of course, got out of the car to take pictures. I, of course, yelled at him, "GET BACK IN THE CAR!" As we look for the wild animal within, it will be tempting to get out of the car and run around looking. But if we sit quietly we will likely get a better view of the scenery as well as the wild animals we are looking for.

ADDICTION AHEAD

As we sit with the Enneagram, eventually we will see a sign not warning about buffalo on the road ahead but warning "Addiction ahead!" The Enneagram, some would say, helps us see our addiction to the lies of the false self. We usually think of addiction in terms of substance abuse. But according to psychiatrist and spiritual director Gerald May, we can also become addicted to the way we look at life. After describing what happens in the human body when it is addicted to alcohol or drugs, Dr. May writes:

> The same kind of cellular (physical) dynamics apply to nonsubstance addictions [as to substance addictions]. If we had been talking about addiction to money, power, or relationships, even if we had been talking about addiction to images of ourselves or of God, we could have said much the same about what happens to our nerve cells.

The phenomenon Dr. May describes can also be seen in the Enneagram. Our Enneagram addictions express themselves in the obsessions we bring into relationships, in our attitudes toward our work, and even in our involvement in church. We are continually faced with the temptation to fixate on our gifts and on our images of self and God. We addictively present ourselves as the manifestation of our gifts rather than manifesting selfless love. We protect ourselves against anything that might tarnish our flattering personal expectations. We are, in short, addicted to ourselves. In the Enneagram we identify this addictive thinking, behavior, and motivation.

David Benner adds another dimension to addiction. He says that "addictions are strategies to avoid human vulnerability and risk." This thought is evidenced in the Enneagram by its underlying assumption that we overplay our gifts in order to hide our weaknesses. Speaking of addiction, Benner says, "What we are most deeply addicted to is trying to escape the limitations of being human by playing God." This is what the Enneagram says also. We are addicted to whatever makes us feel better about ourselves, even if it is not true.

Our addiction to ourselves is perhaps less obvious and more subtle than an addiction to substance abuse. But we can learn much from those who struggle with substance abuse. Like the recovering alcoholic, we become Recovering Ones or Twos or Threes or Fours or Fives or Sixes or Sevens or Eights or Nines. And for each of us, like the recovering alcoholic, we are never completely over our addiction. Knowing the Enneagram will not stop our natural, default reactions to life, but it will help us be aware of these reactions and slow the process. Knowledge of the Enneagram will help us choose between living compulsively to serve ourselves and living in love, offering our gifts to others as God intended in giving them to us.

Let me give a personal example. I take great pleasure in creating a "space," whether it is a room with cardboard furniture for my granddaughter's doll baby or a quiet study where I can write. This certainly reflects the Four love of creativity. When we moved into our current house, I realized in my times of quiet prayer that my calling at the time was to create a physical and emotional space where people could grow closer to God. That sounds a bit lofty. But it's what I wanted to do, and I worked hard at it. It was a life-giving experience for me. Then I went to a Parade of Homes, showcasing builders' best home creations. My own home immediately looked scuffy and inferior. Enter my addiction. First I judged anyone who would spend that much money on a house when people were dying from poverty in the inner city. Then I spiraled into the discouragement and self-loathing of the Four. How could I have thought that I could decorate a living room, much less an entire house? My house didn't hold a candle to the ones I was touring. As I went from house to house, I might have decided that the only way out of my disappointment and embarrassment about my own living room would be to buy more furniture, paintings, and vases to make my home look more like the ones I was seeing at the Parade. But my knowledge of the Enneagram reminded me that I was acting like a Four. That awareness alone loosened the grip of the beautiful homes I had seen. Later, my compulsive thinking gradually subsided, and there settled into my soul a sense that what I had done was good enough. The home I had created reflected my gifts and therefore reflected God. People have since told me that when they come into our home they feel love and peace. That has become good enough for me.

WHERE DO OUR ADDICTIONS COME FROM?

Before we look at the potential addictions of each space, let's look at what the Bible says about the source of our addictive behavior. Scripture, of course, does not use the word *addiction*. But we can see hints in Scripture about where these addictions come from. As Greg Boyd observed in *Repenting of Religion*, "We cannot eat of the Tree of the Knowledge of Good and Evil without becoming addicted to it." In other words, following in Adam and Eve's footsteps, we decide that we will determine what is good and what is bad. We become addicted to the illusion that we know what is good and what is evil. Our addiction is described in living color in our Enneagram space. We are addicted to whatever it is that we have determined is good or right. Likewise, we addictively believe that whatever is the opposite of our choice of "good" is by definition "evil."

Addiction is a strong word. We do not want to hear that we are addicted people. But we cannot deny that we have participated in Adam and Eve's efforts to be the Creator rather than the created. Hints of our addictive choices permeate the Old and New Testaments.

The prophet Jeremiah quoted God saying, "My people have committed two sins: They have forsaken me, the spring of living water, and have dug their own cisterns, broken cisterns that cannot hold water" (Jeremiah 2:13). With an image appropriate to his culture, Jeremiah described what we see in our understanding of addiction. In our addictive behavior we are digging our own cisterns, looking for life in places that don't hold water. Each Enneagram space has a different broken cistern.

Later in his book Jeremiah writes, "Friend deceives friend, and no one speaks the truth. They have taught their tongues to lie" (Jeremiah 9:5). This gets really close to home: in each of our Enneagram spaces we have taught our tongues to lie, about ourselves and about God. We have become addicted to those lies.

Jesus picked up on the theme of lies when he said this about the devil: "When he lies, he speaks his native language, for he is a liar and the father of lies" (John 8:44). When I was in college, our school mascot was a devil. But the devil Jesus is talking about does not run around a football field in red pajamas. This devil is the personification of evil who speaks only lies. And we have inherited many of those lies. They have become the native language of each of our Enneagram spaces. Learning to speak the truth is like learning a second language. It will take years, if ever, before it comes naturally.

ENNEAGRAM ADDICTIONS

Recognizing our Enneagram addictions takes honest reflection and a lot of perseverance. All human beings, on some level, want affirmation, control, and security. The problem is that in our desire for the admiration and affirmation of others, we overplay our gifts and suffer the consequences. When we reach for too much power and control, our relationships suffer. And when we let our fears dominate our lives, we diminish what life has to offer. Our addiction to impressing and controlling ourselves, others, and God leads us right into our Enneagram compulsions: anger, pride, deceit, envy, greed, fear, gluttony, lust, and sloth.

All of these compulsions are the result of the compulsive expression of our gifts. What confuses us is that the gifts themselves are very good. It is our fixation on them and our overuse of them that gets us into trouble. It might help to think of Overeaters Anonymous, the organization created to help those who eat compulsively. It is certainly not that food is bad. The issue this organization is addressing is the compulsive fixation on, or addiction to, food. Translate that perspective to the Enneagram spaces and we can see that it is not that the gift of each space is a danger to us. The danger is in our response to the gift and our addiction to what it offers us, whether it is admiration, control, or security.

The following list is an admittedly oversimplified description of the lies people in each space are tempted to make into addictions.

Ones: The good person who does things very well may become addicted to controlling life to try to make things perfect and to the resulting anger when people or things are not perfect.

Twos: The loving person who is sensitive to the needs of others may become addicted to being needed and be very proud of it.

Threes: The successful person who is indeed very effective may become so addicted to looking successful that he or she chooses to lie rather than admit failure.

Fours: The creative person who lives life to be unique may become addicted to being "different" from everyone else and then begin to think that everyone else has a better life.

Fives: The wise person who looks ahead and creates a vision others can follow may become addicted to gathering information for that vision, hoarding the information rather than using it in love.

Sixes: The loyal person who is admired for being faithful and obedient may become addicted to the fear of anything that looks contrary to rules or authority.

Sevens: The joyful person whom others love for being fun and optimistic may become addicted to all things that bring happiness.

Eights: The powerful person whom people look to for leadership may become addicted to controlling life with his or her own opinions.

Nines: The peaceful person with a gentle, even temperament may become addicted to harmony at all costs, even if it means avoiding helpful conflict.

The Enneagram acts as an "intervention" for us, in much the same way the family of an alcoholic intervenes to encourage the addict to get help. The Enneagram tells us we are not well. We have addictions. We need treatment.

HOLDING OUR GIFTS LOOSELY

Gerald May quotes St. Augustine's observation that "God is always trying to give good things to us, but our hands are too full to receive them." May adds that "our addictions fill up the spaces within us, spaces where grace might flow." This is what I did with my gifts of interior design. I filled my hands with them. Moving beyond God's grace in my giftedness, I became consumed with my gifts. I "needed" for my gifts to be the best. We all face that temptation. Whatever our space, we are tempted to fill up our hands, our lives, with what we think our giftedness should look like. Then we hang on tightly to our gifts. We can't seem to let go. May says that "we may not be able to make our hands completely empty . . . but we can choose whether to relax our hands a little or to keep clenching them even more tightly." Learning to hold our gifts loosely is a lifelong experience. But we are in good company. The Bible tells us that Jesus was "tempted in every way, just as we are" (Hebrews 4:15). The temptations of our addictions are not beyond the grace of God.

We see a glimpse of how Jesus experienced temptation in the account of his forty days in the wilderness (Luke 4:1-13). "Tell this stone to become bread," Satan said. (Could that have been similar to the temptation to fix the problem, faced by those in the heart triad?) Next Satan said, "I will give you all authority." (That would certainly be tempting to those in the gut triad!) And, finally, Satan tempted Jesus to jump down from the highest point of the temple. "For it is written," he said, "'He will command his angels concerning you to guard you carefully; they will lift you up in their hands, so that you will not strike your foot against a stone.'" (I hear something in this that would tempt those in the head triad: using ideas, even those in the Bible, for ego-centered ends.) Others will see different reflections of our Enneagram addictions in Jesus' temptations. But the important thing to notice is how Jesus responded to these temptations. Jesus responded to each one with Scripture, not to support his ego but to speak truth to the lies of the great deceiver.

RESPONDING WITH SCRIPTURE

When we recognize temptation in our own lives, one of the best ways to respond is to stop and see whether there is anything in Scripture that speaks truth to Satan's lies. It will take a lifetime to absorb Scripture in ways that keep it at the fingertips of our hearts, but we can start where we are. Does any passage in Scripture come to mind that might be relevant to this particular temptation? Is there anything that applies to my particular addiction? Can I think of anything in the Old Testament, the Gospel accounts of Jesus' life, or the letters of the New Testament that is similar to what is going on in my life now?

The experience of responding to our addictions with Scripture will look different for everyone. People in each triad will probably have similar temptations and addictions, but those who live in each of the spaces of the triad will have a nuanced experience of that addiction. And, of course, each person in each space will experience the addiction in his or her unique way. We can all learn from each other, but our own addictions will be the most familiar to us. Once again, let me share from my own life, just because it is the one I happen to know the best.

In my own Four space, deeply rooted in the heart triad, I often take on more projects, more obligations, and more responsibility than God intends for me. (I am addicted to impressing people with all that I do.) This is partly because I love to help people, I love to take on creative opportunities, and I love to offer worthwhile service. But I also take on too much because I want people to like me and to think I am special. As a Four I usually respond to my overloaded calendar with anxiety about how I can do everything and guilt about getting myself in this predicament. (Anxiety and guilt are the byproduct of my addiction.) In my prayer time recently, I was so stressed about all that needed to be done, I could scarcely pray. And it was my fault, no getting around that. As I tried to pray, I remembered Jesus' words: "Peace I leave with you; my peace I give you. I do not give to you as the world gives. Do not let your hearts be troubled and do not be afraid" (John 14:27). Those words spoke to my soul. Jesus was offering peace that was different from the world's peace and different from my own idea of peace. I had taught myself to believe that peace comes after all my tasks are done. This is what I had learned from my parents and my culture (and my false self). Jesus was inviting me to listen to real peace rather than the fake peace promised by my addiction. The Spirit of Jesus whispered to my spirit, "Don't be troubled about this. Don't be afraid. I am with you today." For at least a few minutes, I was able to respond to my Enneagram temptations with Scripture.

I will always be tempted to impress people. I will always be tempted by an overactive sense of responsibility. But perhaps I can learn to respond to these temptations as Jesus did: "It is written . . ." That day I remembered it is written that the peace Jesus gives is not the peace the world gives (or that my addiction offers). For all of us, the words of Scripture are a powerful way to respond to the compulsions of our space on the Enneagram. They seep into our soul and gradually change us.

The Enneagram, then, leads me into spiritual transformation by helping me see myself, with my compulsions and addictions, and reminding me that what I am believing may not be the truth. Then the Holy Spirit leads me to the truth of Scripture, and to the freedom of God's love.

FOR REFLECTION AND DISCUSSION

1. How would you define spiritual transformation? What has God used most frequently to invite you into transformation?

2. "We usually think of addiction in terms of substance abuse." But according to Gerald May, we can also become addicted to money, power, or relationships or to images of ourselves or of God. As you review in your mind the three triads or your own space, what addictions does the Enneagram suggest may tempt us?

   How do you feel about the possibility (likelihood?) that you are addicted to your own view of life?

3. "David Benner adds another dimension to addiction. He says that 'addictions are strategies to avoid human vulnerability and risk.'" How do our addictions to our view of life and God seem to offer us protection from vulnerability and risk? What vulnerabilities and risks are most frightening to you?

4. "The prophet Jeremiah quoted God saying, 'My people have committed two sins: They have forsaken me, the spring of living water, and have dug their own cisterns, broken cisterns that cannot hold water' (Jeremiah 2:13)." Spend some time with

this image. Why would the image of a broken cistern work well in the culture Jeremiah was writing about?

What image would work well in our society?

How are our exaggerated gifts "broken cisterns"?

What do you think Jeremiah meant by "living water"?

What is the "living water" God is offering you in this season of your life?

5. What helps you hold your gifts more loosely?

6. "The Enneagram, then, leads me into spiritual transformation by helping me see myself, with my compulsions and addictions, and reminding me that what I am believing may not be the truth. Then the Holy Spirit leads me to the truth of Scripture, and to the freedom of God's love." In your own spiritual journey, how has Scripture helped you embrace truth?

How has something in the Bible spoken to you about your Enneagram addiction?

A Personal Meditation
The Wasting Disease: Psalm 106:13-15

But they soon forgot what he had done
    and did not wait for his plan to unfold.
In the desert they gave in to their craving;
    in the wilderness they put God to the test.
So he gave them what they asked for,
    but sent a wasting disease among them.

These verses tell about a sad thing that happened to the Israelites as they traveled in the wilderness. God had abundantly provided for them when they left Egypt, but "they only cared about pleasing themselves in that desert, provoked God with their insistent demands. He gave them exactly what they asked for—but along with it they got an empty heart" (Psalm 106:13-15 *The Message*).

1. What words would you use to describe your own experiences of the desert and wilderness: *disappointment, despair, fear, anger, self-pity*, or something else?

2. From what you know about your Enneagram triad or space, what are you most apt to "crave" when you are in difficult circumstances? What are your insistent and persistent demands?

3. Can you think of a time in your life when you got what you wanted but it didn't work out very well? See if a time comes to mind that reflects this haunting observation of the psalmist: God "gave them what they asked for, but sent a wasting disease among them."

4. How does the description of your own space in the Enneagram help you understand the risk of your own inappropriate cravings? What grace would you like God to give you to help you not give in to them?

The Enneagram and Transformation

C lose on the heels of my fascination with Alice's question, "Who in the world am I?" is the question, Who do I want to be? How do I become a more loving person? How does change happen in my life? My own journey into the Enneagram has convinced me that I am not who I think I am. I do the right things for the wrong reasons. I am compulsively selfish when I want to be generously loving. I do not know myself as well as I thought I do. Like Alice in Wonderland, I live in a Looking Glass House where everything is backwards.

The Enneagram has been immensely helpful as a mirror to allow me to see things as they really are. I see now that when I thought I was loving, I may have been judging. When I thought I was offering my gifts to serve others, I may have been using them to promote myself. When I thought I knew myself well, I may have been looking only at the person I wish I were. And when I think I need to be more than I am, the truth is that I am complete, made in God's image, and able to love others as God loves me.

But looking in the mirror of the Enneagram is not the end of the journey. I think of the warning of the New Testament writer

James: "Anyone who listens to the word but does not do what it says is like someone who looks at his face in a mirror and, after looking at himself, goes away and immediately forgets what he looks like" (James 1:23-24). James, of course, was referring to listening to the words of Scripture, but his warning is a good one for us as we look at the Enneagram. I do not want to forget what I've learned. I do not want to walk away from the Enneagram without experiencing some changes that grow out of the new awareness it has given me.

I need to ask, then, how does change happen? How can I grow in ways that help me live more out of my true self and less out of my false self, my familiar, default way of being? How can I be transformed in my inner being?

God invites us to transformation in ways that are loving and uniquely personal. But Christian teachers throughout history have identified at least three human experiences that often lead to transformation: suffering, silence, and surrender. Let's take a look at all three in light of the Enneagram.

SUFFERING

Suffering is something most of us try to avoid. But, surprisingly, suffering can be a means to growth. Let me tell you a little story about how suffering works.

When our daughter was about four years old, she should have been sleeping through the night. But regularly we heard the shattering cry, "MOMMY!" I would stumble in to comfort her and encourage her to go back to sleep. I did that night after night until I had had enough. The next night when our sleep was interrupted by the familiar cry, my husband responded. Our daughter did not like the change.

"No! I want Mommy!"

"Well, you got Daddy."

"Then I'm *not* going to cry out anymore."

It worked! We went back to sleep.

The experience with our own adult addictions is a far cry from a four-year-old sleeping through the night. But the rude awakening of our crying daughter reminds me of what happens in my own life. I am unlikely to change my addictive behavior as long as it is working for me. Only when my actions no longer work and consequences of my addictions bring me pain will I think about making changes. This is why suffering is one of the gifts of grace that God gives us to help us begin to move away from our particular addictions.

Suffering can take the form of frustration, disappointment, and discouragement, as well as the times of deep suffering that enter every life. The midnight interchange with our daughter reflects what happens when we are doing something we think will work for us and it doesn't work anymore. The Enneagram teaches us that when we are under stress, we are likely to overplay our gifts. This doesn't work, and it probably takes suffering the consequences to convince us to let go of the compulsions connected to our giftedness. People in each triad are likely to experience this in different ways.

Heart triad people are likely to say yes over and over again to requests for their help until they get so overwhelmed they don't want to get out of bed in the morning. Hopefully their distress will lead them to say to themselves, *I'm not going to do that anymore!* Head triad people will read every book on the subject at hand, ask everyone they know for an opinion, or play mental gymnastics to avoid an unpleasant conclusion. When they run out of options to get *the* answer, they fall into a major funk. Perhaps their frustration at that point will help them let go of looking for security in their planning. And when gut people meet contradiction after contradiction to their own confirmed way of seeing things, they fight back in ways that alienate others. When they see the hurt in those they love, they may choose to soften their ways. For all of us, it is not the affirmation of our gifts but the pain of our addictions that gets our attention.

St. Augustine said, "Seek what you are seeking—but don't seek it where you are seeking it!" Richard Rohr says that in our addiction, we want more and more of what doesn't work. We will keep on going until something so distasteful happens that we register that what we are doing isn't working. For my daughter that meant that crying out at night would no longer work. (Even though Daddy was quite as good as Mommy in daytime hours.) In the same way, we overstate our giftedness in addictive ways until we finally say, "I'm not going to do that anymore!"

That's what I did with the Parade of Homes. The sadness and discouragement I experienced as I went from house to house was familiar. I'd felt that way before. As I mused on that distress, I had to admit that the problem was mine, not that of the builders of the beautiful homes. I could see that my default position (a nice way to say addiction) was to think that I was inferior. To think that I was missing something other people had. And when I saw that truth I said to myself, *I'm not going to do that anymore!* It didn't happen overnight. In fact, that night I lay awake thinking of those beautiful homes. But thanks to my knowledge of the Enneagram, I could at least see what I was doing and begin to let go of my envy, inferiority, and discouragement. Thanks to the love of God, I am experiencing transformation, one day at a time.

NOT ALL SUFFERING IS THE SAME

The "suffering" I experienced that day embarrasses me. As I hear of tragedies around the world, I wonder whether I should complain about anything. It is right to feel deep compassion for others. But it is a mistake to let that compassion become an excuse to avoid the discouragement and suffering in my own soul. God uses our own suffering to lead us to transformation. This is what the Bible promises. The apostle Paul talked about his "thorn in the flesh." "I was given the gift of a handicap," he said, "to keep me in constant touch with my limitations" (2 Corinthians 12:7 *The Message*). He said he prayed three times for God to take it away. God answered him, "My grace is sufficient for you, for my power is made perfect in weakness." Therefore, Paul said, "I will boast all the more gladly about my weaknesses, so that Christ's power may rest on me" (2 Corinthians 12:8-9). Sometimes I think my Enneagram compulsions are my "thorn in the flesh." I've certainly prayed more than three times that they would go away. But God in divine wisdom has allowed me to suffer from the results of these compulsions. This suffering has drawn me into grace and love in ways that strength and success could not.

James, another New Testament writer, wrote to the early church: "Consider it a sheer gift, friends, when tests and challenges come at you from all sides. . . . Don't try to get out of anything prematurely. Let it do its work so you become mature and well-developed, not deficient in any way" (James 1:2-4 *The Message*). We need to be reminded not to try to get out of suffering too fast. It is tempting to look at the Enneagram and assume that now we know the problem and, worse yet, the solution. This is the risk of using the Enneagram for self-management. The Enneagram is about grace, not fixing ourselves. The church father Evagrius warned us, "Do not let the cure to a passion become a passion." When we try to use the Enneagram to fix ourselves, we risk becoming compulsive about whatever it is we think we need to do to change our addictive behavior. Instead, we need to sit quietly, noticing the glimpses of the wild animal within, and patiently ask God to be at work in us, transforming us in love.

SILENCE

Long before I knew about the Enneagram, I had an encounter with silence that was not a happy one. I was a preteen, about ten or eleven. We called them the Double-Digit Years in our house. I remember banging my hands on my pillow and crying out, "God, why won't you listen to me?!" I wanted to know God, to talk with God, to have a relationship with God. But God was silent. God wasn't there. Or so I thought.

In my adult years, I still occasionally metaphorically bang my hands on my pillow and ask God why he's not listening to me. But now I have a better sense of the answer to my question. God is listening. God is right beside me, as he was there for me when I was a child. The problem is that I am too busy talking. Usually I'm talking about all that is wrong with me, with my family, with my world. I am chattering: worrying, planning, pontificating, and complaining.

That's what I was doing a few months ago as I wallowed in a situation that seemed totally unsolvable. (It was the fault of someone else, of course.) In the midst of my negative conversation with myself, I noticed a little whisper, perhaps a glimpse of my shy soul. The whisper brought to mind a passage in Exodus that I have always loved. The Egyptians were pressing down on the fleeing Israelites. It's all recorded in Exodus 14. Talk about negative chattering—the Israelites were really going at it. But I was drawn that day to Moses' words, interrupting their chatter. "Do not be afraid. Stand firm and you will see the deliverance the LORD will bring you today. . . . The LORD will fight for you; you need only to be still" (vv. 13-14). Eugene Peterson in *The Message* translates verse 14 this way: "GOD will fight the battle for you. And you? You keep your mouths shut!" Ahh, yes. That was just what I needed to hear. And it is something I need to hear again and again: just keep your mouth shut.

God gives us the gift of silence, along with the gift of suffering, so that we can be in a place to be transformed. Martin Laird in his book *Into the Silent Land* suggests that when we are silent, we move "from being a victim of what is happening to being a witness to what is happening."

When we spend time in quiet and stillness, we begin to have a clearer view of ourselves and of God. Often when I want to be silent, my mind is chattering on about my plans for the day or carrying on conversations I have had or want to have with others. Sometime I am just fantasizing about who I wish I were or what I wish my life were like. If I cannot silence the chattering, I can at least listen in. When I do that, I notice what is really important to me. Often I don't like what I hear because it is my false self chattering. When that happens, sometimes I can return to the love and grace of God.

Becoming a "witness" to ourselves—noticing our chattering minds—changes how we experience life. We learn to view our thoughts, feelings, circumstances, and relationships in disentangled ways that allow us to not be victimized by them.

The Enneagram invites us to witness ourselves. With its mysterious diagram, it takes us out of ourselves and helps us see our motivation and behavior with more objectivity. If a Two person, for instance, can pull away from her engagements with others for even a few minutes, she may witness her loving actions and see the pride behind them. Or a Nine might realize that the peace he brings to the bargaining table is a gift, but he is using it to avoid conflict rather than reflect the image of God. Or the One might become a witness to the anger that often accompanies her response to anything that is perceived as not good and perfect. Whatever our home space, being a witness to ourselves requires us to be quiet, keep our mouths shut, and listen to ourselves and to our God.

I am a slow learner in the school of silence. Like the disciples in the storm at sea, I often feel buffeted by circumstances I cannot control. I cry out, as the disciples did, "Teacher, don't you care if we drown?" Often, the Spirit of Jesus speaks into my life, "Quiet! Be still!" (Mark 4:35-41). In quiet and stillness I am often surprised that the wind and the waves of my life calm down. Then I remember: Jesus is in my boat. How quickly I forget.

Taking time to be quiet is counterintuitive in our society. At best it might be considered a waste of time. At worst, it is considered lazy. No matter what our Enneagram number, and no matter whether we are living life as a CEO, a pastor, or a young mom, we need to learn to be still for at least a few minutes every day. I had a conversation with a stay-at-home mom who was drowning in busyness. I asked her if she could take five minutes each morning to be totally quiet. She quickly countered with, "Would you settle for one minute?" I've had similar conversations with a lawyer, a professor, and people in the corporate world. It is quite possible that no one has taken me up on the five minutes. But, yes, I'll settle for one minute. One minute—to remember that God is in our boat. And that Jesus would say to the waves of our lives, "Quiet! Be still!" (Mark 4:39). God invites us to rest for even one minute in that peace.

Being alone in the quiet presence of God is as necessary to our spiritual health as sleep and food are to our physical health. I'm not sure transformation can happen without it. But each Enneagram space has its excuses. Those in the gut triad believe they can't take time to be quiet because they might lose their influence and control. Those in the heart triad can't take time to be quiet because they are responsible to fix so many problems. And those in the head triad can't be quiet because that would mean temporarily letting go of their planning and rearranging of life.

WHAT DOES SILENCE LOOK LIKE?

The gift of silence looks different for different people and in different seasons of life. As a very young Christian I spent a few minutes every day in quiet, answering the questions in fill-in-the-blank Bible studies. That didn't last very long. Later I moved into more helpful "quiet times." I studied the Bible and worked through my lists of prayer requests. That worked for many years, and I am forever grateful for those times of absorbing Scripture. Over the years I've spent my times of silence in journaling, centering prayer, contemplative meditation, and with the daily examen. They have all been helpful. The variety of the ways to be silent reminds me that these are not means to get God on our side but invitations to be in the presence of the God who loves us more than we love ourselves.

My sense today is that the most important thing about silence is that these times be intentional and regular. The same is true of exercise. Times of quiet are to my soul what exercise is to my muscles. When I work out, my muscles usually do not feel any different as I leave the gym. But the cumulative affect is noticeable. In a similar way, when I have regular times of quiet, I am strengthening my inner being even though I may not see a difference at first. This strengthening helps me notice when I am living in unhealthy ways, including when I am acting out of my Enneagram compulsions. These times of quiet help me remember throughout the day that God is inviting me to experience love rather than accomplishment.

ALIKE BUT DIFFERENT

Martin Laird says this about what it's like to be silent, or contemplative: "We each make our way on the pathless path of contemplation along different trails, each trail thick with tangled vines of Providence." As my experience of silence is evolving over the years, the Enneagram is helping me notice what seems to be working best for me. Again, this is not prescriptive (saying that this is the way we *should* live) but descriptive (noticing what is actually life giving for us). Let's look briefly at how times of silence might be different for the different triads.

People in the heart triad are very aware of their outer world. They value relationships and they want to help people and fix the problems of the world. They have a free-floating anxiety that they are inadequate, so they try harder and harder to disprove this by doing more and more for other people. People in this triad need to learn to pay attention to the desires of their own hearts. This is why it is especially important for someone in the heart triad to withdraw from others, at least for a short time. A heart triad person needs times every day to sit quietly, alone, acknowledging the deepest desires of his or her heart and resting in the truth that God will lovingly fulfill those desires (Psalm 37:4).

People in the head triad experience silence a little differently. These are people who focus on their inner world, particularly their thoughts. They want to understand everything. And they live with the fear that their personal, inner world will be disrupted and knocked off balance. As they pray, the chattering of their mind pulls them into figuring things out, trying desperately to untangle what is going on in their minds. Letting their prayer become a dialogue with God can be life giving for people in the head triad. If they can silence their pontifications, planning, and fears for even a few minutes, they may be able to listen to what is really going in their souls and talk with God about it. My husband often sits in the backyard—in nature, which is good for head triad people. Sometimes I see him talking to himself. Only he is not talking to himself. He is dialoguing with God, putting his many thoughts into God's gracious, loving hands. When head triad people do this, they are invited to experience peace that "transcends all understanding" (Philippians 4:7).

People in the gut triad have a different challenge as they come into silence. They are aware of both their inner and outer worlds. They thrive on being strong and in control. The idea of silencing this inner drive for even a few minutes can be frightening. They are often high-energy people and need to be very intentional about slowing down to be quiet in God's presence. God invites people in the gut triad to be quiet, still, and alone, not making multiple suggestions to God about how to run the world. They need to just let go and stop worrying about what's going on in their inner or outer world. A very good friend who is in the gut triad has told me many times, as though it were a new discovery, that she needs to just sit. For a few minutes at least, she needs to remember that she is a human being, not a human doing. "Be still," God says, "and know that I am God" (Psalm 46:10 NRSV).

Even though we all have a home base in the Enneagram, we share with each other some aspects of all the spaces. Our times of quiet will reflect God's invitations to all three triads. Sometimes I need to sit and intentionally let go of all the things I think I need to do. Sometimes I need to talk through with God what I am experiencing deep in my soul. And sometimes I need to just sit, not saying or doing anything. These times of quiet lead me to experience a silence that often allows me to hear the gentle whispers of the Spirit (see 1 Kings 19:12).

We can tell when our times of silence are effectively influencing our lives as we begin to notice our responses to people and circumstances become more accepting and less reactive. We are slower to say to ourselves, *That shouldn't have happened to me!* Or, *He shouldn't have done that!* Or perhaps, *I just can't handle this right now!* Instead of this reactive commentary, we begin to see the fruits of the Spirit in our lives: love, joy, peace, patience, kindness, goodness, faithfulness, gentleness, and self-control (Galatians 5:22-23). We don't see them all the time. But when we do, there is often a sense of

"Where did that come from?" It came from the Holy Spirit, who has been transforming us in our times of quiet and silence.

As we practice the discipline of intentional silence at least once a day (whether for one minute, five minutes, or twenty minutes) we will begin to notice that we can enter silence at unplanned and unexpected times during the day. I have a good friend who regularly visits our local prison. One evening there was a delay before she was allowed to go in. "It was great," she said. "I had a chance to sit and be silent before I went in to lead the Bible study." Wow. Prisons are not known to be silent places. But silence was the gift God gave to my friend that night.

SURRENDER

Recovery from our Enneagram addictions includes suffering, silence, and, finally, surrender. Surrender is certainly another mysterious experience. It doesn't look good at first. Surrender to God is frightening to our ego. Augustine said, "All the time I wanted to stand and listen. To listen to Your voice. But I could not, because another voice, the voice of my ego, dragged me away."

Our ego tries to drag us away from surrender. But our ego is not telling us the truth. To the ego, surrender sounds like quitting, giving up. My ego tells me that I am better than everyone else or that I am not good enough, or simply that I cannot possibly be the person I think I should be. Surrender, or detachment from outcomes, allows me to loosen my grip on these lies. Surrender invites us to a deeper love than we have ever known. David Benner says that "from the perspective of the ego, surrender is the squeal of the pig on its way to slaughter. But from another perspective, we can think of it as a birth scream." Jesus said you must be "born again" (John 3:3 NLT). Apparently that new birth may be painful.

THE WELCOMING PRAYER

The Welcoming Prayer is taught by the organization Contemplative Outreach (contemplativeoutreach.org). Although it is not specifically about the Enneagram, it is a good one for our Enneagram journey. It reads, in part, "I let go of my desire for affection, esteem, and approval. I let go of my desire for survival and security. I let go of my desire for power and control."

When we are experiencing the rush of our addictions, the frustrations of our compulsions, or just the unidentifiable anxieties of everyday life, we can pray this prayer. For those of us in the heart triad, letting go of affection, esteem, and approval may be the first to come to mind. Those in the head triad may notice the need to let go of survival and security. And those in the gut triad may notice the need to let go of control. But all of us, several times a day, will notice that we need to let go—of our desire for approval, security, and control.

Sometimes all we can pray is, "Lord, I wish I could let go of my desire for approval, security, or control. I don't even know which one is the problem here." Just pray the prayer. Don't engage with the temptation to fantasize about how to get approval, security, or control—or how to talk yourself out of wanting it so badly. That kind of engagement can be another ego trip. ("I can work this out myself.") The truth is that in the intensity of the moment, I can only cry out for grace. As we share with God our hope and intention, we are surrendering to God's love and letting go of our own efforts to achieve it.

This is the surrender of Mary when she found out that she would be giving birth to God's son: "Let it be with me according to your word" (Luke 1:38 NRSV). It echoes the surrender of Jesus: "Father, into your hands I entrust my life" (Luke 23:46 CEB).

Moses told the Israelites to be still and they would see God deliver them. *Deliverance* may be another word for surrender. As we surrender, God delivers.

The gift of surrender is that we find we no longer need to protect ourselves. We no longer need to do everything we want to do. We no longer need to do everything we think we should do. We no longer need to defend ourselves. This is a lifelong journey. But we are surrendering to Someone who will accompany us each step of the way.

FOR DISCUSSION OR REFLECTION

1. What are some of the consequences of overplaying your own gifts?

   When have you "suffered" from these consequences? What was that like?

2. "The apostle Paul talked about his 'thorn in the flesh.' 'I was given the gift of a handicap,' he said, 'to keep me in constant touch with my limitations.' He said he prayed three times for God to take it away. God answered him, 'My grace is sufficient for you, for my power is made perfect in weakness.'" What are some things in your life that you see as "thorns" or "limitations"?

   How are these things connected to your Enneagram space?

   In what ways have you (or do you wish you had) experienced the sufficiency of God's grace?

3. "Martin Laird in his book *Into the Silent Land* suggests that when we are silent, we move 'from being a victim of what is happening to being a witness to what is happening.'" What is the difference between being a witness and being a victim in our own lives?

   How have you experienced this difference?

   How does knowledge of the Enneagram help move us into a witness position?

4. "Being alone in the quiet presence of God is as necessary to our spiritual health as sleep and food are to our physical health. I'm not sure transformation can happen without it. But each Enneagram space has its excuses." What experiences have you had with being silent?

If you are inclined toward silence, what "excuses" does your false self offer for not spending more time in silence with God?

5. "Recovery from our Enneagram addictions includes suffering, silence, and, finally, surrender. Surrender is certainly another mysterious experience. It doesn't look good at first. Surrender to God is frightening to our ego." How do you define surrender to God?

Why might surrender be a frightening term to our ego or false self?

6. "I let go of my desire for affection, esteem, and approval. I let go of my desire for survival and security. I let go of my desire for power and control." How do you respond to this prayer?

Spend some time praying this prayer in silence.

A Personal Meditation
Crucified with Christ: Galatians 2:20-21

I have been crucified with Christ. My ego is no longer central. It is no longer important that I appear righteous before you or have your good opinion, and I am no longer driven to impress God. Christ lives in me. The life you see me living is not "mine," but it is lived by faith in the Son of God, who loved me and gave himself for me. I am not going to go back on that. (The Message)

1. Take a few minutes to be quiet and open to the love of God. Take several very deep breaths, remembering the Spirit is the Breath of God, always breathing new life into your inner being.

2. "I have been crucified with Christ. My ego is no longer central." This is a truth that we are still in the process of experiencing. How does your knowledge of the Enneagram help you embrace this truth?

3. "It is no longer important that I appear righteous before you or have your good opinion, and I am no longer driven to impress God. Christ lives in me." As you reflect on what you have learned about yourself from the Enneagram, how would you write this verse to describe yourself?

4. "The life you see me living is not 'mine,' but it is lived by faith in the Son of God, who loved me and gave himself for me." What do you think it means that "the life you see me living is not 'mine'"? How do you experience this in your own life?

5. What difference does it make to you today that your ego is no longer central and that God loves you? Try to express this in a short prayer.

Continuing the Journey

The Enneagram is a mirror for the soul. Sometimes, quite frankly, when I look in the mirror, all I see is the discouraging image of my false self with its self-serving compulsions and its addictions to illusion. Other times in the mirror of the Enneagram I see my true self, the gifted, free self who is able to love unselfishly and unconsciously. Usually I see a blurry mixture of both. But I also see grace. Grace draws me away from illusion into the truth of God's love for me.

The week after we were engaged I received a note from Bob's mother. "Dear Alice," she wrote. "I have been praying for you since Bob was a baby. It's as though I saw in a mirror darkly and now I see you face to face." She was, of course, referring to the words of 1 Corinthians 13:12 where Paul compares our spiritual journey to looking in a mirror. At first the reflection is not very clear. When Bob was a baby, Bob's mother had only a vague impression of the woman she hoped Bob would marry. When she met me, I am sure I was quite different from what she expected, but to my astonishment, she loved me. In a similar way, when I look at myself in the mirror of the Enneagram, I do not always see clearly, and I have only hints of the person I am becoming, but to my astonishment, I am loved by God more than I could ever imagine.

TRANSFORMATION BEYOND INFORMATION

Now it is time to look beyond the information the Enneagram gives us into the mirror of self-awareness and growth. The information of this amazing paradigm is not enough for me. I need ongoing experiences of awareness and transformation. The place I look for this is in Scripture. As I continue my Enneagram journey, I keep my Bible open. The self-awareness the Enneagram gives allows me to read Scripture in a more personal, reflective way. This means that I experience what the author of Hebrews wrote to the early church: "the word of God is living and active; . . . it is able to judge the thoughts and intentions of the heart" (Hebrews 4:12 NRSV). The Enneagram has given me a head start in knowing the thoughts and intentions of my heart. This has helped me be open to the ongoing process of transformation through the words of the Bible. "Your word," says the psalmist, "is a lamp to my feet and a light to my path" (Psalm 119:105 NRSV). This is what I need—not just a map, but Someone to light my way.

This kind of transformational experience is not efficient. We see only as much as we can handle in each season of life. Even Jesus did not tell the disciples everything they needed to know at once. "I still have many things to say to you, but you cannot bear them now. When the Spirit of truth comes, he will guide you into all the truth" (John 16:12-13 NRSV). As the Holy Spirit reveals truth to us, we participate in a continuing journey of transformation. Knowledge of the Enneagram increases our self-awareness and helps us journey on.

But the ways we engage with the Word of God are varied, according to our needs, gifts, temperament, and, dare I say, Enneagram space. Many people learn biblical truths through Sunday sermons. Others read devotional books. For many of us, our engagement with Scripture is through personal and group Bible studies, where we analyze verses and events of Scripture using our analytical, reasoning abilities to get at the basic meaning of the passage. Sermons, devotions, and analysis are all important, but I would like to suggest two ways of reading Scripture that lend themselves well to the awareness that knowledge of the Enneagram gives us.

LECTIO DIVINA

One way is lectio divina, an ancient way of approaching Scripture. It is slow, personal, and reflective. Thelma Hall in *Too Deep for Words* says that when she approaches Scripture in this way, she reads a few verses and spends time absorbing their truths for her life. She says, "I choose a text—preferably short—and read it slowly, listening to it interiorly with full attention. . . . My goal is to personalize the words, to real-ize them, as God is speaking to me, now." She goes on to say that in this way of reading, "what we hear may be more than the words in themselves convey. The Spirit who vivifies them is himself the meaning, expressed through the words even more than by them."

Lectio divina in its classic form is described with six Latin words: *silencio, lectio, meditatio, oratio, contemplatio,* and *incarnatio.* I will give a brief description of this experience, but for an excellent, expanded description see *Opening to God* by David Benner.

We start with *silencio,* a few minutes of silence where we let go of the immediate cares of the day and open ourselves to whatever God has for us in our reading. *Lectio* is the reading part. It is good to read the verses at least twice, probably out loud one of those times. Then comes *meditatio.* We think and muse about what the verses say. *Oratio* is when we respond to God, telling God the feelings we had as we thought about the verses. Then *contemplatio,* when we listen to God. This is when the Holy Spirit "vivifies" the Word in our hearts. What thought or feeling or perspective does this passage give me about my life today? We are silent. The Spirit whispers to us. And finally, *incarnatio*, where we notice how God might be inviting us to apply the truths of these verses to our inner being or our outer activities.

Some people journal their thoughts and responses. Other people draw pictures of their experience. Still others sing. You might even take your knowledge of the Enneagram and notice how the perspective of your home space influences your receptivity to the Scripture. The goal here is to be quiet, to listen, and to hear how the Holy Spirit is guiding us into truth, just as Jesus promised.

ENTERING INTO THE STORY

Another way of engaging with Scripture is rooted in Ignatian spirituality, taught by Ignatius of Loyola, an early church father of the sixteenth century. Irene Alexander, a psychologist and spiritual director, describes how we can experience transformation through this way of reading. She suggests that we enter into the stories of the Bible and read them with an emotional dimension, "to imagine what this person must have been feeling and to find the part of myself that identifies with that emotion." As we imagine what the person in the story is experiencing, this focus "enables our heart, God's spirit within, to lead us to a story that fits the challenge we are experiencing."

Engaging with Scripture this way fits well with our study of the Enneagram. Just as we view our everyday life through our own particular Enneagram stance, so we will read the Bible with a particular point of view. Knowledge of the Enneagram, and specifically knowledge of our own triad or space, will help us engage with Scripture in a more personal way. Sometimes I see my own compulsions in the lives of the people I read about. Sometimes the gifts of my triad help me understand more about the problems they might be experiencing. Learning the Enneagram has deepened my self-awareness, and that awareness has enabled me to look at

Scripture in a more lively, living way. I can "hear" in ways I have not heard before.

Lectio divina and Ignatian spirituality may look a bit frightening to those who are more familiar with a cognitive, linear way of reading Scripture. These approaches are very personal, reflecting an intimacy with God that is, indeed, too deep for words. But we do not need to be afraid we will miss the truth. We have Jesus' promise to the disciples that "the Advocate, the Holy Spirit, whom the Father will send in my name, will teach you all things and will remind you of everything I have said to you" (John 14:26). And we have Paul's reminder to the church at Philippi: "Let those of us then who are mature be of the same mind; and if you think differently about anything, this too God will reveal to you" (Philippians 3:15 NRSV).

Far from missing the truth, when we read Scripture in this personal way, as well as in an analytical, historical way, the Holy Spirit will whisper truth to our hearts and minds in the perfect way for each of us to hear. With this in mind, I have decided to take the risk of allowing you to listen in on one of my own recent experiences in the Gospel of Matthew. This engagement lasted for a long time, coming to mind again and again over several months. My experience with the passage reflects both lectio divina and Ignatian spirituality. You will be able to see how my heart triad perspective and my Four stance influenced me as I engaged with this passage over several months.

PETER WALKING ON WATER: A PERSONAL REFLECTION

I looked up this passage after several different people, over a period of a few days, happened to mention the story of Peter walking on water. It was a familiar passage. But when I hear something mentioned several times in different contexts, I try to take notice. Perhaps it is an invitation from God. In this case, it was.

Here is what I read when I looked up the passage.

Immediately Jesus made the disciples get into the boat and go on ahead of him to the other side, while he dismissed the crowd. After he had dismissed them, he went up on a mountainside by himself to pray. Later that night, he was there alone, and the boat was already a considerable distance from land, buffeted by the waves because the wind was against it.

Shortly before dawn Jesus went out to them, walking on the lake. When the disciples saw him walking on the lake, they were terrified. "It's a ghost," they said, and cried out in fear.

But Jesus immediately said to them: "Take courage! It is I. Don't be afraid."

"Lord, if it's you," Peter replied, "tell me to come to you on the water."

"Come," he said.

Then Peter got down out of the boat, walked on the water and came toward Jesus. But when he saw the wind, he was afraid and, beginning to sink, cried out, "Lord, save me!"

Immediately Jesus reached out his hand and caught him. "You of little faith," he said, "why did you doubt?"

And when they climbed into the boat, the wind died down. (Matthew 14:22-32)

The first thing I wondered about was what Peter might have been thinking and feeling in his boat that night. Peter's trip on the lake, into the storm, was Jesus' idea. Jesus "made the disciples get into the boat." Then Jesus went up to a mountainside to pray. This did not make sense to me. When I am in trouble, I want Jesus in place helping me, not off having a quiet time. Even if Jesus went to the mountain to pray for the disciples, it was still his idea for them to go out on the water, and they were the ones battling the waves. It all seemed quite backwards to me, the reversal of what I thought should happen. If I had been Peter, I might have cried out, "Jesus, why did you send us out here?!"

Soon after my initial engagement with this passage, my husband came home from a difficult meeting. As we walked the dog in the park, he told me about his frustrations and I "helped" him by making multiple suggestions. (That's in my job description as a heart triad person.) As we walked and talked, I could tell it wasn't working. All of a sudden, I heard a thought in my head: *It's not your boat.* Oops! Perhaps Jesus had allowed Bob to go out into a storm, and here I was trying to fix it. I spent several days walking around saying to myself, *It's not your boat!*

In my prayer, I found myself asking, "If it's not my boat, what am I supposed to do with the sadness and frustration I feel watching this boat toss around in the sea?" As a Four, I focused on the storm. It overwhelmed me. In answer to my question, I seemed to "hear," *Join me on the mountain.* Ah, yes. That was God's invitation to me. To join Jesus on the mountainside. As I was with Jesus, I might pray for Bob, but the particular invitation was to be with Jesus myself. To find comfort in his presence, his wisdom, his love. In other words, focus on Jesus, not the storm.

But the story goes on, mine as well as the Gospel story. Soon after I was invited to the mountain to be with Jesus, Bob and I went to visit one of our daughters and her family. Any parent knows that there are lots of storms and waves in the lives of our children. I knew that I was going to be visiting a whole sea of boats that were not mine—my daughter's boat, my grandchildren's boats, even (truth be told) their dog's boat. This would be like a final exam for the transformational class called An Introduction to Not My Boat. As we drove to their house, I hoped I might get a passing grade.

It was more difficult than I thought. Not only did I face the heart triad's unfounded sense of responsibility to fix everything, I also experienced my Four desire to be special by offering to help in creative ways that other people could not. I could feel the accompanying melancholy that often comes with the realization that I cannot do the things my false self says to do. I decided to confess my concerns to my daughter and told her I was trying not to get in her boat when I didn't belong there. But I'm her mother, for heaven's sake. Didn't she want her mother in her boat? "Well, yes," she said. "I do like you in the boat with me, but don't pick up the oars." Next invitation from God: *you don't need to pick up the oars.* (I'm still working on responding to that invitation.)

In the meantime, I've gone further into the passage. Next up, I joined Peter trying to walk on water. What in the world would that be like? For me, walking on water means not sinking into the deep, dark feelings of melancholy that are always crouching at my Four door. It means not jumping in to fix something that is not mine to fix. It means not taking everything so personally. It means not believing that everyone else has abilities and qualities that I am missing. It means not giving in to the compulsions of my false self. Doing this for even a few minutes seems as impossible as walking on water. It is counterintuitive. It is scary. But God is inviting me to let go of the lies of my Enneagram space. God is inviting me to walk on water.

No, I say, *I can't do that.* God replies, *Try it, just one step.* So, like Peter, I experiment, one step at a time. I start to sink, forgetting to disbelieve the lies. Jesus reaches out to catch me, but even his words "Oh, you faithless person. Why did you doubt?" are hard to hear. In the tone of voice of my false self, Jesus' words sound something like this: "What is wrong with you? Can't you even believe?" The truth is that Jesus' words were spoken to me with the love of a parent: "I know you are having a hard time believing. Someday you will look back and know that you did not need to doubt."

Finally, I do what Peter did. I climb into the boat with Jesus. *And the wind dies down.* That is where I am today. Four months after I started musing on this passage, I am living with the truth that when Jesus is in my boat, the wind ceases. Every day I am trying to remember that.

My engagement with Matthew 14 is certainly different from what yours would be. These reflections are not the same as a typical Bible study or the teaching of a sermon. What I look for is a synergy between the many ways of experiencing Scripture. This personal approach to reading the Bible opens me to hear the Holy Spirit apply specific, subtle, and mysterious truth to my own life at the times I need to hear it.

FOR REFLECTION AND DISCUSSION

1. "Jesus did not tell the disciples everything they needed to know at once. 'I still have many things to say to you, but you cannot bear them now. When the Spirit of truth comes, he will guide you into all the truth'" (John 16:12-13). How do you experience the Spirit of truth guiding you into more truth?

2. When have you embraced a truth that you realize you could not have learned at an earlier time in your life? Does this seem like a grace to you or a waste of time?

3. What words describe your experiences of reading the Bible? Interesting? Exciting? Confusing? Guilt-producing? Fun? What are your own words?

    What experiences have you had reading the Bible in a lectio divina way or in an Ignatian way?

    What do you like about these approaches to Scripture?

    What questions do you have?

4. Whether you are on your own or with a group, you might want to take time now to engage with the following meditation on Mark 10:46-52. What is it like for you to read the passage in this reflective way?

A Personal Meditation
Bartimaeus Meets Jesus: Mark 10:46-52

Jesus and his followers came into Jericho. As Jesus was leaving Jericho, together with his disciples and a sizable crowd, a blind beggar named Bartimaeus, Timaeus' son, was sitting beside the road. When he heard that Jesus of Nazareth was there, he began to shout, "Jesus, Son of David, show me mercy!" Many scolded him, telling him to be quiet, but he shouted even louder, "Son of David, show me mercy!"

Jesus stopped and said, "Call him forward."

They called the blind man, "Be encouraged! Get up! He's calling you." Throwing his coat to the side, he jumped up and came to Jesus. Jesus asked him, "What do you want me to do for you?"

The blind man said, "Teacher, I want to see."

Jesus said, "Go, your faith has healed you." At once he was able to see, and he began to follow Jesus on the way. (CEB)

1. As you read this passage slowly, notice who in the passage catches your attention the most: Jesus, Bartimaeus, the disciples, the crowd, or the people who scolded Bartimaeus? How do you identify with the person or people you noticed?

2. If you had been the blind man, what feelings do you think you would have had sitting by the road when Jesus walked by? How would you have responded to those who criticized you? How would you have responded to Jesus calling you out?

3. If you had been one of the ones who scolded Bartimaeus, what judgments would you have had when you saw what he was doing?

4. Think about a stressful circumstance or relationship in your own life today. If Jesus said to you, "What do you want me to do for you?" how would you answer?

5. What blind spots in your own life surprised you in your study of the Enneagram? Write a prayer asking God to heal your blindness and give you sight.

Epilogue

Answering Alice

D id Alice ever get the answer to her question? I'm not sure,
but I know I still love to ask, "Who in the world am I?" Only
God knows the final answers. But thanks to the Enneagram, I
know a little more than I did when I started this journey.

And, thanks to the Enneagram, I am changing. Alice in Wonderland wondered if she had been changed in the night. "Let me
think," she said. "Was I the same when I got up this morning? I
almost think I can remember feeling a little different." I too think
I remember feeling a little different today than yesterday. Thanks
to God's transformational grace, I can celebrate almost imperceptible changes. And thanks to my knowledge of the Enneagram, I
can give words to the experience. And I know that when I look in
the mirror and see things I don't like, I can embrace my imperfec-
tions and know that God's love meets me there.

I am thankful for the mirror of the Enneagram. It reflects truth
to me. It helps me see ways I would like to change. It leads me to
grace. My journey of the Enneagram has taken me not to Wonderland but into the embrace of a loving God.

Acknowledgments

In the oral tradition of the Enneagram I have absorbed the perspectives of many authors and teachers. I am forever grateful for their influence in my life and my understanding of the Enneagram.

In particular, I think of Richard Rohr and Suzanne Zuecher, whose books I have read and reread, eaten and digested. Their words have become an integral part of my own perspective on the Enneagram. The writings and teaching of Jerry Wagner, as well as Don Riso and Russ Hudson, have influenced me deeply. As I have written about the Enneagram here, I have acknowledged their contributions wherever I can. But I have absorbed so much more from them than I can credit in the endnotes. I am grateful for all of those authors and teachers who have been in my own circle of oral (and written) tradition.

Some of the material in this book was first included in *Conversations Journal* 12, no. 2 (Fall/Winter 2014): 22-26.

I am also deeply grateful to my colleague Jessie Vicha. Jessie and I have journeyed together into the Enneagram as well as across many miles teaching workshops together.

And I am thankful to those who responded to my request for feedback and for personal interviews on their experiences with the Enneagram: Sandy Alcorn, Miriam Blank, Steve Dome, Lana Gentile, Jeanie Griffin, Susan Groah, Anita Lustrea, Gail Minkus,

Tania Mitton, Suzanne Nies, Barbara Perry, Mary Reimer, Linda Richardson, Mary Kay Richardson, Ewan Russell, Donna Scott, Alice Siehoff, Win and John Stanford, Marilyn Stewart, Don Vicha, Christina Walker. And thank you to my family, especially Bob, Dorie, and Elisa. I've been interviewing you for years, perhaps without you even knowing it. Thank you for all you have given to me, in so many ways.

Using the Enneagram in Spiritual Direction

B efore we leave our study of the Enneagram, I would like to look at its value in spiritual direction. Both the Enneagram and spiritual direction seek to lead us into deeper self-awareness, which, in turn, leads us deeper into grace.

First, a word about spiritual direction. Spiritual direction is a relationship between two people who look together for the direction of God in one of their lives. Spiritual direction goes back to the desert mothers and fathers and was preserved in the Catholic Church. In recent years, Protestant churches have discovered the benefit of this wonderful ministry.

In spiritual direction, one person is the director and the other the directee. These designations are a bit misleading, but they help us embrace the difference between spiritual direction and other conversations we have with counselors, friends, and fellow believers at church. The director in spiritual direction has received training to listen well and to ask questions that prompt the directee to notice desires, compulsions, and relationships in ways they might not have noticed before. The director does not "direct" the directee about the issues they are discussing. The director gently directs the directee to listen to the Holy Spirit who is revealing truth and love. The director creates a quiet space where the directee can listen.

HEALING FOR THE WOUNDED SOUL

Some say a spiritual director is like a midwife to the soul. Others compare the director to "the physician of a wounded soul." Author Tilden Edwards has this to say about that comparison:

> And what does a physician do when someone comes with a bleeding wound? Three things: He or she cleanses the wound, aligns the sundered parts, and gives it rest. That's all. The physician does *not* heal. He or she provides an *environment* for the dominant natural process of healing to take its course.

Like a physician, the spiritual director provides an environment for healing. But in spiritual direction the healing is the healing of the soul. It is usually imperceptible at first, and it takes a long time. The reason spiritual direction is a healing experience is because the director listens. To listen to someone is to love that person. And love heals.

I am a spiritual director, but I am also a directee when I go to see my own spiritual director. The image of the physician to the soul helps me as I think of going for spiritual direction myself. It reminds me that I want to describe my symptoms well, but I want to go with an open mind about the observations my director might make. When I go to my doctor with a sore throat, I don't tell him I have a bacterial infection and please give me an antibiotic. Nor do I assume I have a viral infection and just need to take two aspirin and go to bed. I want him to know my symptoms, check out what he thinks is going on throughout my body, tap into the wisdom of his medical training, and tell me what he thinks is happening.

My job as a directee is to be as honest and clear as I can be about what is happening in my life and in my relationship with God, with myself, and with others. It doesn't help to say, "I am just a mess." Or, "Everything is fine, thank you." I need more grist for the spiritual direction session. The self-awareness that comes from my knowledge of the Enneagram gives me more clarity as I try to describe to my spiritual director what is going on in my life.

ENNEAGRAM BENEFITS FOR THE DIRECTEE

For me, this self-awareness is often related to my own Four space as well as what I know about the heart triad. I may want to explore why I am so distressed about a relationship where I feel I have disappointed someone. (That would have been my last session.) Or I may want to look at why I am so stressed doing all the creative things I love to do. (That would have been the appointment before last.) And often I need to look at how my own shame and self-doubt is influencing me. (That would be a lot of sessions.) All of these questions and issues overlay my relationship with God. What do I do when I feel I have disappointed the God who loves me? How do I discern what I believe God is inviting me to do? Why am I plagued with self-doubt even though I do not believe it is what God wants for me? These questions are often rooted in blind spots in my life. I don't know why I do what I do or why I think what I think, let alone why I feel what I feel. The Enneagram helps me make intelligent guesses at what questions I might ask.

But the Enneagram does more for me. The Enneagram, with its wings and arrows, helps me see where I might want to go. I can talk with my spiritual director about how to access the experience of serenity, the gift of the One. That is still a mysterious gift for me. I need someone else to reflect back to me what it would be like to have that strange experience of believing that I am okay and that life is okay. Sometimes I can celebrate with my spiritual director when I notice that I am not succumbing to my arrow space of desolation, or when I am embracing the gifts of my wing spaces. It is good to have someone savor those moments with me.

Over the years, I've noticed that even if the spiritual director I am meeting does not speak the language of the Enneagram, it is still immensely helpful for me to know myself and to be able to put that self-awareness into words. The Enneagram also gives me questions to ask to explore more deeply whatever the topic is that I am bringing to the direction session.

QUESTIONS FROM THE ENNEAGRAM

If spiritual direction is new to you, or if you are still learning the language of the Enneagram, let me suggest some questions that might grow out of the perspective of each space of the Enneagram. These questions are generic; they need to be applied to real-life situations. And, of course, those real-life situations are the real topic of conversation, not whether or not they fit into some place in the Enneagram.

The following list of questions is designed to help those in each of the nine spaces access a perspective about your life that you might want to bring to your spiritual director. You don't want to address all of these questions in one session, of course. These are just thought starters. As I prepare to go for a spiritual direction session, I spend time thinking over my recent life and noticing what circumstances and relationships have the most impact on me right now. I bring those to the appointment. Often my knowledge of the Enneagram helps me express a little more clearly the issues I am bringing to the spiritual direction conversation.

Number Ones. People in the One space might want to look for areas where they are doing things really well, where they are using their gifts of goodness to enrich the lives of those around them. Spiritual direction is a good place to celebrate that.

Ones might also want to notice areas of unhealthy perfectionism in their lives as well as places where they expect others to be perfect. And they will probably want to talk about the times when they are angry. What is that all about? Where are the areas in life where you experience the most melancholy (the Four arrow)? When do you have fun (the Seven arrow)? How do the characteristics of your wing spaces (Two and Nine) influence you for better or for worse?

As Ones think about the grace of serenity, they might ask themselves, *What feelings do I have about the possibility of accepting life rather than reacting to it? And what difference would that make for me?*

Number Twos. People in the Two space will probably want to celebrate relationships and activities where they find that they are really helpful to people. How do you feel about that? Tell your spiritual director about the joy you have in loving others.

In the safe environment of spiritual direction, Twos may want to address the pride in their lives. How do you see pride sabotaging your efforts to love those you are close to? How willing are you to let others know your needs?

Looking at the arrows and the wings, Twos might want to think about relationships where they see others backing away. When are you apt to become manipulative and be too assertive about helping (the Eight arrow)? What do you do in your life that is creative and life giving for you (the Four arrow)? And how does the perfectionism of your One wing affect you? How about the drive for success of your Three wing? What about your wings serves your gifts of love well, and what distracts from your gifts?

Probably at some time, Twos will also want to talk about humility. What is humility? Do you like the idea of being humble, or do you resist it? Where does humility show up in your life these days?

Number Threes. People in the Three space love to be effective. Celebrate your successes with your spiritual director. What do you have to celebrate this week?

What happens inside you when you feel like you've failed at something? When are you most likely to feel the temptation to deceit, which the Enneagram says is your compulsion? How do you feel about that? What happens in your soul when you get overextended in your drive for success? Looking at the arrows and the wings, notice times in your life when you are tempted to drop out and become a couch potato (your Nine arrow). When is that most likely to happen? And, on the positive side, what is it like for you to experience the loyalty and the courage of the Six space? How do the characteristics of your Two and Four wings influence your life?

How do you feel when you speak the truth, either to yourself or to others? In what ways does truth feel like a grace to you?

Number Fours. People in this space have been given the gift of creativity. In what ways do you express your creativity? Celebrate this and let your spiritual director in on the pleasure you have in expressing this gift.

In what relationships are you aware of envy? Is that a blind spot for you or something you're often aware of? How does the typical melancholy of the Four affect you? In what areas of your life do you feel you are missing out on what others have? In what ways are you tempted to give in to the overly helpful patterns of your Two arrow space? And how would it feel to you to experience the invitation of your One arrow space to accept things as they are and to live with what is rather than react against it? How do the characteristics of your Three and Five wings influence you?

How do you respond to the grace of equanimity—the ability to notice your melancholic emotions without getting stuck in them? Does that sound like a grace or an impossibility to you?

Number Fives. People in this space are wise people. How do you see yourself as wise? In what areas of life are you most apt to express your wisdom? Be sure to let your spiritual director know when you are enjoying this gift and giving it to others.

How do you experience the greed that tempts Fives? Do you experience this mostly with the knowledge and information you collect or in other areas of life? How do you know when you have enough knowledge or information? If you begin to act like your Seven arrow space, exaggerating pleasure and ignoring pain, what is that like for you? And, in contrast, what is it like for you to pick up the good characteristics of your Eight arrow and lead with confidence? Do you identify more with your Six wing or your Four wing?

What do you think about the idea of being detached from your gifts, holding your wisdom loosely? Does that appeal to you? Why or why not?

Number Sixes. Loyalists, in the Six space, are faithful people. Tell your spiritual director about your pleasure in being loyal and faithful in your relationships. How do you do that? Let your spiritual director know about your gifts of loyalty.

You will probably also want to talk about your fear, the compulsion of the Six. What things are you most afraid of? How do you usually respond to your fears? How might spiritual direction help you in this area of your life? How does the desire for effectiveness and success of your Three arrow space affect you? How do you feel when you go there? And what is it like for you to go with the flow, as suggested by your Nine arrow space? How does that feel? Which wing influences you the most in your current life circumstances, Five or Seven?

When do you experience courage in your life? How would you like to be more courageous? What evidence is there that God has given you the grace of courage?

Number Sevens. People who are Sevens are full of joy and enthusiasm. What do you like about being that kind of person? How do you see joy as a gift you give to others? Celebrate this with your spiritual director.

What happens inside you when there are things in your life that are clearly not joyful? How do you attempt to collect more and more experiences that might hide any unhappiness in your life? Where does that kind of gluttony lead you? What might help you deal with the sad things you experience as you live life? When are you most likely to fall into the control and perfectionism of your One arrow space? And how does the wisdom and thoughtfulness of your Five arrow space help you? What do you like and dislike about your Six and Eight wings?

Sobriety is the grace given to Sevens. What does sobriety mean to you? Can you think of a time recently when you have experienced sobriety? Is there an area in your life now where you would especially like to experience sobriety?

Number Eights. Eights are usually leaders and strong challengers. What do you like about being in leadership? How do leadership roles bring out the best in you? How have you used your leadership for good? Share these experiences with your spiritual director.

What happens when people contradict or disagree with you? How do you feel and how are you likely to respond? If leadership opportunities are denied you, or taken away from you, what do you do to try to get them back? How do you see yourself wanting more and more power? How do the endless observations of your Five arrow space tempt you to overthink relationships and circumstances? When do you have opportunities to use your power in the loving, helpful ways of your Two arrow space? Do you identify more with the characteristics of your Seven wing or your Nine wing? Which do you like better?

Innocence is the grace given to Eights. What comes to mind when you think of innocence? How is it for you when you can approach a situation without expectations and judgment? Do you experience grace in that stance?

Number Nines. Nines give peacefulness to our world. How do you see yourself contributing peace in your family? At work? In your church? In your neighborhood? Celebrate your gift of peace with your spiritual director.

How do you feel about conflict? Try to think of a relationship in your current life where you are trying to avoid conflict. What do you do in your desperate effort to keep peace? When are you most tempted to drop out and give up on your capacity to deal with a situation? What is that like for you? How do you hide behind the loyalist stance of your Six arrow space? If you move to change things for the better, as people in your Three arrow space would do, what would that be like for you? How do the characteristics of your Eight and One wings affect your life?

What kinds of things look like "taking action" for you? How do you experience the Nine grace of action? When have you taken action and experienced something life giving as a result?

LISTENING TO THE ENNEAGRAM IN SPIRITUAL DIRECTION

As you muse on these questions (remember, not all at once!), see what stands out to you about your life and spiritual journey that you would like to talk about with a spiritual director or close friend. Then take the risk of doing just that.

If you don't have a spiritual director and would like to find one, the best place to look is to ask someone who is already meeting with a spiritual director. See if someone you know can give you some leads. If not, perhaps your church or another church in your area has a spiritual direction ministry. Sometimes this is listed on the church website. Another source for spiritual directors in your area is Spiritual Directors International at sdiworld.org. All spiritual directors are a little different. Their way of offering spiritual direction reflects their own spiritual tradition and orientation as well as their personal style. After you find one or two names, call or email them and ask about how they practice spiritual direction. What is their spiritual perspective? How often and where do they meet with people? Is there a fee? Dialogue with each possible director and see whether you sense a spiritual and relational fit. You will probably want to set up an initial appointment to see whether the relationship will work for you. If not, keep looking.

ENNEAGRAM BENEFITS FOR THE SPIRITUAL DIRECTOR

There is a reason the roots of the Enneagram go back to the desert mothers and fathers. It provided a paradigm to help them listen well to those who sought out their counsel. It does the same for spiritual directors today.

By far, the most helpful benefit of the Enneagram for a spiritual director is the self-awareness it offers. I am convinced that we cannot be effective spiritual directors without knowing ourselves and embracing all that is good and all that is not so good about who we are. When I meet with someone for spiritual direction, I am not shocked or put off by their temptations and struggles. I know from my own Enneagram space that I too am deeply tempted by the lure of my own false-self perspectives and, in particular, by the compulsions of my own Enneagram space. The Enneagram invites me in no uncertain terms to extend mercy to those I meet with.

I am grateful, then, for the awareness the Enneagram gives me about my own life. But I am also grateful for the ways the Enneagram has given me a bit more clarity as I listen in on other people's lives. Let me suggest a few ways this happens.

The true self and the false self. The Enneagram reminds me that we all live out of a true self and a false self. We all have blind spots. We are all confused about who we really are. When I sit with people in spiritual direction, I often hear them say that they just don't understand why they do what they do and why they feel what they feel. Sometimes it surprises me too! Then I remember that we all have an inner critic, a false self telling us lies, a voice that is contradicting the voice of love. With that perspective, I can begin to ask questions that may help them think twice about the masquerade of the false self, as well as the giftedness of the true self. The Enneagram helps me know what questions to ask.

Getting a perspective. Sometimes the Enneagram helps me even when I don't know the home space of the person I am companioning. I often hear characteristics of a particular Enneagram space in what they tell me. But like my doctor, I dare not jump to conclusions. I need to hold it loosely, ask questions carefully, and do what I can to help the person see new personal truth. Unlike the doctor, I try not to pronounce a diagnosis. That is up to the directee as he or she listens to the Spirit of God. But knowledge of the Enneagram helps me think of the diagnostic questions I might ask.

The triads of the Enneagram. I rarely talk about the Enneagram as I meet with someone for spiritual direction unless they too know the language of the Enneagram. But in my mind, as I listen, I look for characteristics of a particular triad. The triads help me keep it simple, so I am not distracted by trying to place someone in a particular space.

Is this person sounding like a heart triad person? If so, then relationships are very important, or at the very least, relationships are important in the issue the person is presenting. I can guess that they care a lot about what other people think. And there is a good possibility they struggle with shame. With that in mind, I ask gentle questions that might help them see truth about themselves they might be missing. I might ask: Are you feeling responsible to fix the problem of this person you love? How is the opinion of others influencing the choices you are making in this relationship? How might a sense of shame about yourself be holding you captive in this situation?

Or, if the person seems to be speaking out of a head triad position, I prepare myself to listen well and patiently as they tell me what they think about the situation at hand. Then I might ask them to identify one or two feelings they have about that situation. I might ask what they fear about the situation. Is it because it requires a new, uncomfortable perspective for them? Or do they fear going against the opinion of someone they love? Sometimes they can name the fear. Sometimes it just helps to know it's there.

If I hear hostility or anger in what the directee is saying, I might guess they are in the gut triad. I do not pigeonhole people, but I ask questions I might ask of someone in the gut triad. I could ask whether they can think of another relationship or situation that has really irritated them. What are the similarities and dissimilarities to what is happening now in their life? I might ask how they would like to change the situation. I might even ask how the desire for control is influencing them.

Truth be told, I can ask all of these questions to most people. At one time or another, all of us experience very similar temptations. But the triads of the Enneagram give me a head start in knowing what questions might be most helpful.

The witness of the Enneagram. God invites us to be a witness to our lives rather than a victim. We've already established how the Enneagram helps us witness our lives in ways that reveal our blind spots as well as our gifts. As a spiritual director, I see my role as coming alongside those I listen to, helping them clarify what they are witnessing.

If the person I am companioning is familiar with the Enneagram and knows his or her space, this opens up a whole vista of things we can look at. I try to resist the temptation to make assumptions about the directee just because I know his or her space. But I do use my knowledge of the person's Enneagram space to ask questions. Is this what you are experiencing? What particular temptations of your space are you struggling with? What would it feel like to receive the grace offered to those in your space?

Before I plunge in to the Enneagram, I usually ask if it would be okay to explore some of its insights. I don't want to get distracted by the Enneagram if it's not helpful at this time. I will occasionally ask, "Is it okay with you to have an Enneagram moment here?" Usually they say yes, but if not, I go where they want to go.

HOW WE SEE LIFE

Transformation is not so much about becoming better and better people. It is more about how we see ourselves, our relationships, and our life circumstances. In transformation, these patterns of looking at life change ever so slowly and often without our knowing they are changing. The privilege of the spiritual director is to watch that closely but from the outside. The Enneagram is one tool to enrich the experience of transformation, and it is a gift to those of us who have the privilege of watching God's grace at work.

Additional Resources

THE ENNEAGRAM

Books

Renee Baron and Elizabeth Wagele, *The Enneagram Made Easy* and *Are You My Type, Am I Yours?*

Loretta Brady, *Beginning Your Enneagram Journey*

Ian Morgan Cron and Suzanne Stabile, *The Road Back to You*

Janet Levine, *Know Your Parenting Personality*

Helen Palmer, *The Enneagram* and *The Enneagram in Love and Work*

Don Richard Riso, *Enneagram Transformations*

Don Richard Riso and Russ Hudson, *The Wisdom of the Enneagram*

Richard Rohr and Andreas Ebert, *The Enneagram: A Christian Perspective*

Clarence Thomson, *Parables and the Enneagram*

Diane Tolomeo, Pearl Gervais, and Remi J. DeRoo, *Biblical Characters and the Enneagram*

Jerome Wagner, *The Enneagram Spectrum of Personality Styles*

Suzanne Zuecher, *Enneagram Spirituality* and *Using the Enneagram in Prayer*

Digital Resources

Richard Rohr, *The Enneagram: The Discernment of Spirits*

(May be ordered from Center for Action and Contemplation, PO Box 12464, Albuquerque, NM 87195, or www.cacradicalgrace.org.)

Websites

enneagraminstitute.com (Consider requesting a free daily quote about your home space. Follow the prompts at this website to "enneathought.") enneagramworldwide.com

BOOKS ABOUT THE SPIRITUAL JOURNEY

Irene Alexander, *Practicing the Presence of Jesus*
Ruth Haley Barton, *Invitation to Solitude and Silence*
David Benner, *The Gift of Being Yourself* and *Soulful Spirituality*
Greg Boyd, *Repenting of Religion*
Alice Fryling, *The Art of Spiritual Listening*
Thelma Hall, *Too Deep for Words*
Judith Hougen, *Transformed into Fire*
Martin Laird, *Into the Silent Land*
Gerald May, *Addiction and Grace*
Richard Rohr, *Falling Upward*

BOOKS ABOUT SPIRITUAL DIRECTION

Jeannette Bakke, *Holy Invitations*
Alice Fryling, *Seeking God Together*
Margaret Guenther, *Holy Listening*

Notes

⌒〜

CHAPTER 1: WHAT IS THE ENNEAGRAM, AND WHERE DID IT COME FROM?

8   *the exact origins of the Enneagram*: Don Richard Riso and Russ Hudson, *The Wisdom of the Enneagram* (New York: Bantam Books, 1999), 19.

9   *three great overwhelming spiritual experiences*: Richard Rohr, *The Enneagram: A Christian Perspective* (New York: Crossroad, 2002), 22-24.

19   *Nearly all wisdom we possess*: John Calvin, *Institutes of the Christian Religion*, quoted by Carolyn Nystrom in *John Calvin: Sovereign Hope* (Downers Grove, IL: InterVarsity Press, 2002).

Lack of awareness is the ground: David Benner, "Brokenness and Wholeness," Dr. David G. Benner (blog), June 3, 2016, www.drdavidg benner.ca/brokenness-and-wholeness.

CHAPTER 2: THE TRUE SELF AND THE FALSE SELF

28   *at the core of the false self*: David Benner, *The Gift of Being Yourself* (Downers Grove, IL: InterVarsity Press, 2015), 70.

33   *Self-acceptance gives assent to be who I am*: Judith Hougen, *Transformed into Fire: An Invitation to Life in the True Self* (Grand Rapids: Kregel, 2002), 121.

41   *only a crack that separates the past from the future*: Suzanne Zuercher, *Enneagram Spirituality* (Notre Dame, IN: Ave Maria Press, 1992), 10.

44   *The false self may become paralyzed*: Ibid., 11.

45   *they instinctively "dig in"*: Ibid., 12.

CHAPTER 4: THE HEART TRIAD

66 *envy causes Fours to see everyone as stable*: Don Richard Riso and Russ Hudson, *The Wisdom of the Enneagram* (New York: Bantam Books, 1999), 191.

Equanimity is a spaciousness of the heart: Russ Hudson, *Laughing and Weeping*, DVD (Albuquerque, NM: Center for Action and Contemplation, 2009).

CHAPTER 5: THE HEAD TRIAD

79 *The Generalist: The Hyperactive*: Don Riso, *Enneagram Transformations* (Boston: Houghton Mifflin, 1993), 85.

immersing themselves in constant activity: Ibid.

if they run out of stimulation: Ibid.

81 *learn to stay with each experience*: Ibid.

83 *presuppose a world in which there isn't enough*: Clarence Thomson, *Parables and the Enneagram* (New York: Crossroad, 1996), 7.

CHAPTER 6: THE GUT TRIAD

87 *a childlike capacity to experience each moment fresh*: Jerome Wagner, *The Enneagram Spectrum of Personality Styles* (Portland, OR: Metamorphous Press, 1996), 112.

you do everything to excess: Ibid.

CHAPTER 8: UNDERSTANDING THE WINGS AND THE ARROWS

106 *think of the wings as neighbors*: Loretta Brady, *Beginning Your Enneagram Journey* (Allen, TX: Tabor Publishing, 1994), 94.

CHAPTER 9: BIBLICAL TRUTHS REFLECTED IN THE ENNEAGRAM

121 *We are not satisfied being God-like*: Greg Boyd, *Repenting of Religion* (Grand Rapids: Baker, 2004), 68.

CHAPTER 10: ADDICTED TO OURSELVES

131 *if we want to see a wild animal*: Parker Palmer, *Let Your Life Speak* (San Francisco: Jossey-Bass, 2000), 7-8.

132 *The same kind of cellular (physical) dynamics*: Gerald May, *Addiction and Grace* (San Francisco: Harper & Row, 1988), 83.

132   *addictions are strategies to avoid human vulnerability and risk*: David
        Benner, *Human Being and Becoming* (Grand Rapids: Brazos, 2016), 15.

        What we are most deeply addicted to: Ibid.

134   *We cannot eat of the Tree of the Knowledge*: Greg Boyd, *Repenting of
        Religion* (Grand Rapids: Baker, 2004), 221.

137   *God is always trying to give good things*: May, *Addiction and Grace*, 17.

        we may not be able to make our hands completely empty: Ibid., 19.

CHAPTER 11: THE ENNEAGRAM AND TRANSFORMATION

146   *Seek what you are seeking*: Augustine, quoted in Richard Rohr, *What
        the Mystics Know* (New York: Crossroad, 2015), 30.

149   *we move from being a victim*: Martin Laird, *Into the Silent Land*
        (Oxford: Oxford University Press, 2006), 81.

151   *We each make our way on the pathless path*: Martin Laird, *A Sunlit Ab-
        sence* (Oxford: Oxford University Press, 2011), 55.

152   *People in the heart triad are very aware of their outer world*: Suzanne
        Zuercher, *Using the Enneagram in Prayer* (Notre Dame, IN: Ave
        Maria Press, 2008), 15-20.

        These are people who focus on their inner world: Ibid., 21-25.

153   *aware of both their inner and outer worlds*: Ibid., 11-14.

154   *All the time I wanted to stand*: Augustine, quoted in Laird, *Sunlit Ab-
        sence*, 41.

        surrender is the squeal of the pig: David Benner, *Soulful Spirituality*
        (Grand Rapids: Brazos, 2011), 157.

CHAPTER 12: CONTINUING THE JOURNEY

161   *listening to it interiorly with full attention*: Thelma Hall, *Too Deep for
        Words* (Mahwah, NJ: Paulist Press, 1988), 36-37.

        expanded description of lectio divina: David Benner, *Opening to God*
        (Downers Grove, IL: InterVarsity Press, 2010).

162   *to imagine what this person must have been feeling*: Irene Alexander, *Prac-
        ticing the Presence of Jesus* (Eugene, OR: Wipf & Stock, 2011), 12, 21.

APPENDIX 1: USING THE ENNEAGRAM
IN SPIRITUAL DIRECTION

174   *And what does a physician do*: Tilden Edwards, *Spiritual Friend*
        (New York: Paulist Press, 1980), 125.

Other Books by Alice Fryling

The Art of Spiritual Listening: Responding to God's Voice Amid the Noise of Life

Disciplemakers' Handbook: Helping People Grow in Christ

A Handbook for Engaged Couples (with Robert A. Fryling)

Parenting with Purpose and Grace: Wisdom for Responding to Your Child's Deepest Needs

Seeking God Together: An Introduction to Group Spiritual Direction

IVP BOOKLETS

Seven Lies About Sex

Spiritual Compatibility in Dating

Too Busy? Saying No Without Guilt

formatio
TRADITION. EXPERIENCE. TRANSFORMATION.

Formatio books from InterVarsity Press follow the rich tradition of the church in the journey of spiritual formation. These books are not merely about being informed, but about being transformed by Christ and conformed to his image. Formatio stands in InterVarsity Press's evangelical publishing tradition by integrating God's Word with spiritual practice and by prompting readers to move from inward change to outward witness. InterVarsity Press uses the chambered nautilus for Formatio, a symbol of spiritual formation because of its continual spiral journey outward as it moves from its center. We believe that each of us is made with a deep desire to be in God's presence. Formatio books help us to fulfill our deepest desires and to become our true selves in light of God's grace.